Kem Luther

COTTONWOOD
ROOTS

University of Nebraska Press
Lincoln and London

© 1993 by the University of Nebraska Press

Manufactured in the United States of America

The paper in this book

meets the minimum requirements of American

National Standard for

Information Sciences – Permanence

of Paper for Printed

Library Materials, ANSI Z39.48-1984

Library of Congress Cataloging-in-Publication Data

Luther, Kem, 1946–

Cottonwood roots / Kem Luther. p. cm. Includes

bibliographical references.

ISBN 0-8032-2906-2 (cl. : alk. paper) 1. Luther family.

2. Middle West—Genealogy.

3. Frontier and pioneer life—Middle West.

4. Country life—Middle West.

I. Title. CS71.L973   1993   929'.2'0973—dc20

92-44167 CIP

For

Jeni & Erin,

the next to wonder

If I am going to die, I would like to know it.

I have many things to say, and it will

take some time to say them.

– Horace Mann, dying of
what was presumed to
be typhoid fever
in 1859.

Contents

Crawford County

Erie County

Sources

Custer County, Nebraska

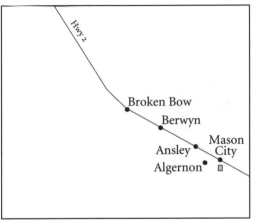

⊞ CEMETERY

Broken
Bow

The gravel crunches as I pull from the driveway onto the blacktop. It is a frigid morning. Signs of last night's frost are everywhere, from the hoar on the stubble in the south field to the cracklings of fine ice assaulting the windshield from bases at the corners. The cold stored in the plastic mass of the steering wheel seeps out to numb my fingers. But the forecast on the ten o'clock news last night promised some warmth. It is a good day for beginnings.

Two journeys start today from this driveway. One moves in the spatial domain—although it will carry me in all physical directions, most of its moves will be on a horizontal plane, west to east, along the lay of the land, from this ranch in Broken Bow, Nebraska, at the near edge of the American desert, to the fields of New England. Its vertical moves are small compared to the horizontal—so small on a trip so long that the vertical motion is almost insignificant. I will be dropping about 2,000 feet in half as many miles. We might as well give thought to the undulations on the skin of an unblemished tomato as to assign meaning to the ups and downs of this journey. I remember reading that if the earth were the size of a tomato we would regard it as perfectly smooth. Sensitive fingers would not find the crenulated Rockies on its skin. And the density of the reduced earth, if kept consistent with its reduction in size, would be that of a ball of wet mud. If we could find a place to poise the earth, standard gravity would flatten it like an overripe tomato. But this earth-as-tomato image doesn't work itself into any physical reality on this trip: from my place and perspective, perched on a system of concrete highways, earth will be hard—or hard enough—for the journey. Even a spring thaw, that great dread of earlier trippers in these lands, will not pose much of a hindrance.

The second journey is in the dimension of time. Or at least in the dimension of time that is the past. The displacement from one end of this trip to the other, the move from now to a point in the past, will be less than 200 years. But to move in time is a traveling, not unlike what I am doing in this car. Talk of time invariably uses the words of space. We don't know how to talk about time in any consistent way without referring to moves in a spatial dimension. We say that time *flies*, that some event *arrives* unexpectedly, that the day *creeps* along. Time is marked in miles. Our days are numbered like signposts, our nights are encampments. So I will combine the two journeys, since language will scuttle any attempt to hold them apart, and use the unassigned vertical dimension of this trip—the up and down—to encode the time-related aspect of these travels.

The only problem is whether we go *up* or *down* when we go back in time. I can see both mappings. Time advances. Advancing is going forward, forward is progress, and progress is up, so time in its natural migration goes up. Tracing it into the past will take us *down*. But other images imply that forward is down. Time rolls along, slips away, and carries us off as a river moves its flotsam to the waiting sea. These depictions say down, and the countermove on my part would take me *up*. Choose one mapping, and lose the power of the other image. But for this voyage in time one image commands the other. The destination of this movement in time is an earlier place on the family tree. Trees grow upward. Searching for roots takes you down. So time in this conceptualization moves naturally to the top, and we, traveling backward in time, travel down. It may help that the real vertical dimension, the one being ignored, is also down a little. The drop is not a lot, though; we won't be doing much coasting.

In the days ahead I will follow a line of testimony where it leads. At the end of the line is an ancestor. I'm off in this cold morning, fumbling with the heater switches, seeking the way to a person. A book of maps on the seat beside me shows the roads to my destination. But I don't really know my destination, not in the sense of putting my finger on one of the maps and saying "Here it is." My destination is more a person than a place, and to get to that person I have to go through another person, and another, and each person in the line can only point me vaguely on. The situation reminds me of those eighteenth-century immigrants who boarded a ship in Rotterdam with a letter of introduction to someone in the Colonies. "To Theophilus Miller," the letter in a waterproof oilskin says, "in the new land." They arrived with only the hope of Christian hospitality, asking at each leg of the journey to be pointed in the right direction. I am going to the old world, to the old and civilized East, but the drop in time takes me to a social frontier. I am going down in time, with hardly more than a name as a letter of introduction. Friends will be where I find them, but I have hopes. You don't do genealogical work for long before you learn how much you need friends and inns of hospitality and pointers to the road. If you have to know exactly where you are going before you leave, you do not go.

This is not a research trip. I think of what begins today as more of a pilgrimage. A pilgrimage, someone once said, is *purposeful traveling*. But that definition can't stand without qualification. Pilgrimage is also traveling without purpose. It depends on what we call purpose, on whether we see purpose as something we have too much or too little of. Our daily lives are full of many purposes. I will go here, and do this, then I will go there, and do more. But these smaller purposes crowd out larger goals. We have a nagging sense that the quest for what is attainable undercuts the search for what is sublime. "In the long run," says Thoreau, "men hit only what they aim at. Therefore, though they should fail immediately, they had better aim at something high." We have purposes, but lack Purpose. A pilgrimage, then, is a time when a larger purpose is deliberately allowed to suspend small demands. I set my eyes on the horizon, on an encounter. I will visit a shrine, honor a saint, do contrition at a holy place, take the waters of healing. And as I frame the larger purpose, the smaller ends lose their hold on my consciousness. Large purpose, instead of giving me even more goals, frees me from small masters. I don't know exactly how to get to the new goal. I don't know whether some path will take me closer or not. Almost any event can be in the construction of the way. Common happenings acquire new meanings. We open ourselves to new experiences which were ruled out by the short distance between means and end in our mundane purposing.

The goal in the days ahead is to visit the roots of a family. The name at the far end of this family is Ebenezer Luther. In the early decades of the nineteenth century Ebenezer and his wife, Aurilla Wait, set off from family and friends in New York State to join the line of Americans and Europeans moving west over the withdrawing frontier of Indian lands. On the way they grew a new family of their own, a large one. But somewhere on the way the new family lost track of the older family. Ebenezer probably wondered how that other, disassembled family in the East fared, what crops they harvested, and what children they reared. Ebenezer's descendants wonder who they were.

I met Ebenezer and Aurilla in the early 1980s. On a typed and copied and recopied set of pages, called by my relatives the "Luther Family Tree," was the opening paragraph

Ebenezer Luther, of Dutch and English parentage, birthdate unknown.
Aurilla M. Wait, born April 10, 1801, English, a native of New York State.

From this austere and absolute beginning the family history went on to describe the birth, loves, and death of a thousand persons. I could trace there my own line, through Ebenezer and Aurilla's son Henry to my own grandfather Arthur, and from grandfather to me. The genealogy itself had been the painstaking work of a succession of aunts over a period of sixty years. The first ones wrote down what they knew, what their parents had told them, what they found in the family Bibles. The following generations of family historians copied what was known, wrote letters, held reunions, and tried to preserve a sense of belonging to an extended family. I didn't know, when I first read this family history, that I would join these weavers of families. I remember reading the first lines over and over, and wondering why so little was known and preserved about this Moses who had led us into the open air of the Great Plains. Not even a single story, a single anecdote or personal reflection, graced the page containing those opening lines about Ebenezer. I wanted to know, and with that spark of curiosity the desire that brings me out this morning was kindled. I lean toward the steering wheel, my breath fogging the top of the windshield.

The family history, this line of ancestors stretching from here to New England, will be my safety rope. Most readers of local history are aware of the staked cords that were used in the Midwest to allow farmers to get to and from their livestock in the winter. The blasting, blinding winds of these parts could turn a fall of snow into a danger to anyone who had to walk a few hundred feet in it. Livestock needed to be tended every day, so the trip to the barn had to be made, storm or no storm. It was possible to lose one's way in the hundred yards between house and barn. To wait out the blizzard on the open land would be to die of exposure. You could not count on being found in time: sometimes individuals only fifty feet apart could not see or hear each other. To set off walking, however, might mean moving farther away from the shelter of the homestead, since there was no way to tell in what direction you were going.

I do not know what highways of the spirit I will travel. There is a danger that I could lose my way in the conceptual storms. As long as I can see the ancestral line in the family history, however, I know where my purpose lies. If I cannot see the larger end, if I cannot turn like the needle of a compass to the direction in which I should go, I can always hand-to-hand it down the line of ancestry, son to father, until I have regained my sense of direction. All my attention does not have to be dedicated to navigation. This is why the trip can be a pilgrimage. And, like Chaucer's pilgrims, I am at liberty to tell a story or two. The serendipity of the pilgrim journey is an important part of it. The lack of concrete evidence, the ultimate fear of the researcher, is the blessing of the pilgrim. It gives him room to tell the tale.

With a twist of the wheel I put the car on State Highway 2, headed into Broken Bow. No other cars in sight. How many thousands of times have I made this trip? I could probably close my eyes and drive to town. Our ranch is a little over a mile from the edge of town. Broken Bow was a significant place when I was growing up here in the fifties and sixties. It may have had 5,000 people at one point. To many this place would be pure rural America, the edge of the wilderness, but to me it was civilization. A *little* town was a town like Berwyn, or Ansley, or any of a dozen diminutive hamlets within a twenty-mile radius, towns that had seen a half-century of decline, from a few hundred souls down to the handfuls some of them have today. We pitied the people living there. But today we are objects of pity to the bigger cities on our driving horizons. About the time I left high school the change began to happen, and Broken Bow, which had grown for fifty years by feeding on the corpses of the surrounding towns, itself became food for larger towns just an hour's drive away, veritable metropolises with populations of 20,000 and more, whose football teams could not even be allowed to play against our little towns with their limited resources. We became victims of the change in mental space induced by the expanding road system.

Roads. Who would have thought that good roads could have such a bad effect? What politician has ever campaigned on a platform of poorer roads? And yet the destruction of the roads is probably the one thing that could save this town from economic ruin. Or something equally drastic which would have power to reconstruct the mental distances that have doomed towns like this. There is a place on the other side of Broken Bow called Westerville. Westerville, when I last saw it in the sixties, was a sad street with some decaying houses. Yet Westerville and Broken Bow vied with each other in the late 1800s for the honor of being the county seat. What happened to Westerville was what didn't happen to Westerville: the railroad didn't come through it. Westerville was condemned to perish at the moment some Railroad Intelligence looked at a map and drew a line that missed the town by five miles. The railroad meant life and money and commerce and people. It came to Broken Bow, and we prospered. Westerville, severed from the life-giving steel vine, withered. The lucky ones sold and got out early. When the railroad finally began to lose its hold on the land, modern roads came in to replace it. And these roads came through Broken Bow, following the line and spirit of the iron right-of-way. So Broken Bow, first trained to the ways of the overland horse and wagon, managed to live, even to thrive, through two transportation revolutions. But then some fool of an Easterner plotted an interstate system that missed us by sixty miles. If there is anyone left in Westerville they must be laughing.

These declining towns in Nebraska aren't like the ghost towns from the mining days. They were not bustling places of commerce one year and five years later abandoned. They die in little bits, on a long logarithmic scale. The half-life is about thirty years. Every thirty years, the town has about half of what it had. In the beginning of the decline, the loss is hard. The passenger trains cease, the bus service dies, properties go down to a construction-cost baseline, vital businesses leave, and healthy businesses get replaced by long rows of gift and resale shops. In the end they reach the lower parts of the scale where the changes are not so obvious from one year to another. Sometimes the half-life of the decay even lengthens. Any number of factors can change this. One of the more obvious factors is being in commutable distance to a town that is growing. Failing that, there aren't many safety nets. I've heard that in Comstock, about forty miles from here, you can buy a house for 2,000 dollars. They don't even have a grocery store.

I pass through Broken Bow. For my father and his brothers and sisters this has been *town* (as in the phrase "I'm going to town") for sixty years. I know the western facades on the businesses around the square as though they were my own skin. When I was ten, our teacher brought us down to the square for an afternoon to sketch the rows of storefronts. I drew part of the north side of the square. I found that picture a few years ago. Only one of the stores was still there under the same name, and I'll wager they weren't doing the same level of business. My father saw the change on the other side. When he first came here with his father—it was in 1895, I think—Broken Bow was a jumble of houses and a few stores. It wasn't his town then: his was Mason City, Nebraska, which I'll pass through twenty-odd miles from now. But he came here, to the county seat, when there was need, several times a year. In the 1920s he moved here and opened a general store that specialized in buying cream and hides. For most of his years he saw the town change through constant growth. I have seen it under the waning moon.

Outside of Broken Bow the road turns and the town disappears almost instantly. You can tell which towns are not in decline yet. They have long stretches of strip developments caused by the slow crawl of the towns along the main arteries of travel. I can imagine what the Appian Way must have looked like at the height of the Roman Republic. But after some years of stagnation and retraction, the edges become acute. It's country to city in a few hundred yards this morning, and I am suddenly wrapped in the rural landscape of central Nebraska. The scenery slides by. My next stake on the safety line is in Mason City, half an hour ahead. By the time I get there I will have dropped back almost a hundred years. I will not be descending at this rate again. I feel like I really could coast. My foot twitches above the brake.

Perhaps I should have lingered in Broken Bow. There was so much more to tell. But I am drawn away. The point of a pilgrimage is to go a place whose presence is largely spiritual. Pilgrims do not see the rapacious clerics, the beggars, and the vendors of sordid trinkets. The reality of Broken Bow is too much for me now. If it had been my end, and not my beginning, I might have seen it with the eyes of faith. My ancestors surely did. It was their hope, not their malice, that orphaned me at the edge of the world.

Mason
City

My grandfather lives in the time of myth for me. He is far enough from the world I regard as real that a visit to him on this pilgrimage does not compromise its spiritual tone. Although I knew him on this side of myth, he has become more ancestor than person to me. I was only five when he died. For the last few months of his life our home was a kind of hospice for him, equipped with strange devices usually associated with nursing homes. They say he taught me to read the newspaper in those solitary months, waiting to die. He was winding down his life, wrapping himself tight in his memories, just I was unwinding, my mind beginning to open itself to the world outside my house and yard. I like to think he was responsible for a lot of that opening, that the door that was closing and the door that was opening was, for a brief moment, the same swinging door.

I'll be driving by Mason City in a few minutes. I'll turn off the highway there and look for the city cemetery. This is not a stop to record dates or to sift through documents. There are no documents there to consult. The neoclassical dogma of local government which rules between Ohio and the Pacific Ocean says that land corners are square and records are deposited in county courthouses. This is still Custer County (it is one of largest counties in the Midwest), so the records are back in Broken Bow. I'm not totally at the mercy of those written records, however. We are still on the edge of living memory, in the mere shallows of the past. I can look up and see the surface of the present several decades above my head. If I went knocking on doors in Mason City I could probably find people who knew my grandfather.

Mason is a town far advanced in pursuit of half-lives. Few stores in the old three-block business district are doing any business. It has been many years since money was spent to renew the faces of the emporia. Mason City has always looked to me like a town from one of the Western films that were my regular Saturday afternoon fare as a child. One expects to see board sidewalks and hoop skirts, and smell the manured mud of the streets. If I walked behind the store faces I would not be surprised to find scaffolding, and see costumed extras rushing between boom mikes and cameras.

The oldest county maps don't show Mason. They show a place called Algernon about three miles to the west. The Mason City part came with the railroad. It was decreed that there should be a depot and train stop every five to seven miles when the rail was laid through here in the 1880s. Mason was the name of some railroad engineer. He probably penciled a stop on a map and gave it his name. A lot of towns got named that way. What little development was happening at Algernon halted when they didn't get the depot, and Mason City became the town of note in this township. Eventually Algernon (at the family picnics it was pronounced al-JER-nun) became the designation for a country school rather than the district. The school is now gone, and the name will probably follow it unless it can attach itself to something more enduring.

As I drive down the main street toward the corner of Mason City that has the cemetery, I am struck by the inconsistency of the fifty or sixty houses left in town. Directly beside a natty little house with the *au courant* yard bric-a-brac and the latest in large wooden butterflies are houses of eye-catching squalor. I have heard that Indians come down from the Rosebud Reservation in South Dakota and rent these houses as a place to live during seasons when the rural economy lurches from its usual stagnation. It's shelter, I guess. This isn't a place I would put money into a house I was renting.

The cemetery is surprisingly hard to find. I know it is at the edge of town. The trick is to find the one road in this maze that leads over the hill hiding the cemetery. There is no one around to ask. Perhaps that's just as well. There is a lot of Yankee blood in the Midwest. I can see it coming. "Can you tell me how to get to the cemetery?" "You have to die first, son." I am spared the bad joke, however. I have found the poorly maintained road that mounts the hill to the cemetery.

My father used to bring me here every few years. I suppose it was on Memorial Day. He would tell the same stories he had told in previous years, pacing around the cemetery like a farmer walking bounds on his property. It was many years before I realized that Dad hardly *knew* anyone here personally. No adult Luthers are buried here, for one thing, just people who married into the Luthers in my grandfather's prime. The stones of the other families Dad used to point out—the Amsberrys, the Dadys—are mostly the stones of the generation before Dad's own. The ones that Dad knew as friends, the children of the ones buried here, did what Dad did. They left Mason, and are buried, many of them, in the Broken Bow cemeteries. These were people who were important to Dad, the ones he respected as a child, but they were not his companions. It would be as if I hauled my children around the Broken Bow cemetery thirty years from now: there wouldn't be a lot of my friends there—they will be buried from here to the ends of the earth—but I would know the families. I was impatient with Dad's desire to range the whole cemetery, to step it off.

It was a ritual my father was performing, a ritual that was hidden to the impatient child in tow. As a gesture of placation to the spirits of the dead in this place my father was assuming the position of his own father in order to address the dead as companions. He was apparently required to approach them on their own terms, as one of them, as a contemporary. And out of politeness to them he walked the borders of their land and surveyed their domains. Heaven knows, my father professed no religion, respected little of civic ritual, and had no particular appreciation for graveyards in general. How he reached inside himself to find this primitive rite I do not know. So much of his life was subconscious. Thinking about him and these cemetery excursions, I am struck by how little I really knew about him.

I park the car on the untended grass and walk toward a familiar row of three gravestones. I suppose that I am in my own way making the same appeasements to the spirits of my ancestors. I am assessing their habitations, visiting quietly, coming in the guise of someone who understands their sufferings and their hopes. Perhaps the motivation of people who observe this rite is not altogether altruistic: to honor the dead is also to try to make them satisfied with their place, to deny them horrifying access to our own land. They must not, above all, be allowed to break forth among the living. I think I will never be able to attend a funeral without seeing it as a set of programmed rituals designed to set boundaries for the dead, to pray that they will be firmly on their way, and not turn back to confound the comfortable realm of the living. This is a deep feeling. Religion must either promote this sentiment or fight it as superstition. It cannot be neutral without dismantling part of its own foundation. Though I can take refuge in the objectivity of genealogy, I don't always feel safe in these places.

The stones I am standing in front of now were placed here by Dad after he had earned enough to lift himself out of the dire day-to-day poverty of pioneer farming. They mark the graves of his mother, his mother's sister, their father, and Dad's infant brother: every person in my grandmother's family who came to Nebraska, except my father. The story of how they came to be here I know from oral tradition. The tradition is direct enough, and comes to me from so many sources, that I have no reason to doubt it. I have backfilled it with some research, though, and have checked the essential details. It is a story with a keen of high sorrow, sharp enough to cure deafness. It was told to me in bits and pieces, each small enough that it could be said quickly before the catch in the throat and the burning in the eye ended the tale. It took Dad a lifetime to tell me what he knew about it, and it wasn't even his story. It was more his father's experience, explained to him as he grew, until it was a piece of his own existence.

Arthur, my grandfather, was a boy of fourteen when his family homesteaded in Algernon in the 1880s. Homesteading is a simple idea: you move onto land, improve it, and after a while it is yours for a nominal fee. Sounds like an unqualified boon to the pioneer. Through the better part of the period of regular homesteading, however, all of the security and most of the profits were on the side of the government and the railroads. Settlers on the freshly vacated Indian lands were led to believe that the government wanted to make them *producers*, and that they would become rich entrepreneurs. What the government really wanted to do was to create a society of *consumers*. To be sure, Andrew Jackson complained in the 1830s that the U.S. government's income from the western lands was a net loss, but, even if it was true for that decade, it was the last time it was true until the modern era. With a little priming of the pump the homesteading acts returned generous profits for Eastern money.

Some of the last of the reasonably good and farmable lands to be taken under the U.S. homesteading acts were here in Algernon. There was still land available for years afterward, however. My father was able to homestead in the Nebraska Sandhills in 1916 under the Kincaid Act. To this day, I understand, property is still there for homesteading on the margins of the world. So the land taken in the 1880s was not the last of the free land; but it was the last of the land that could support a tightly packed, self-sufficient farming community on the model of, say, eastern Pennsylvania or central Ohio. Even then, it could only do it in scattered areas along the river valleys. The settlers in the westward expansion were not unaware of the problems with this land. They were, after all, farmers, with an eye for the weather and a knack for the soil. They knew that when you traveled west the annual rainfall decreased as you came under the rain shadow of the western mountain ranges. In the early days of the expansion, as newcomers moved into the lands across the Alleghenies, the regions over the Missouri River were called the "Great American Desert." It took a major publicity campaign by the government and the railroads to convince the wary public that there was rain over the river. The campaign succeeded, however. About the time of the Civil War, when large tracts of trans-Missouri land were opened up for settlement, the land-hungry came in droves. Local land offices did the business they became a byword for. But the homesteaders knew there was a line out there where the rain ended. It was, unfortunately, not well marked on the maps. We know today that this line twists its way through the heart of Nebraska like a rattlesnake. In the wetter years in the 1880s it looked like the line was around Broken Bow. In the first few years the rains came as required. Settlers subscribed to fanciful theories about how plowing land and laying telegraph lines could improve the rainfall patterns. But when the droughts of the nineties came it was clear that the snaking line was a sidewinder, and that the line of rainfall could shift unpredictably eastward to lands bordering the Missouri River.

It was to a tenuous homestead in this fickle land that Arthur came with his parents and thirteen brothers and sisters in the year 1884. Later I'll drive out to the homestead site. For now the gravestones hold my attention. Under one of these stones are the bones of Ella Etta Ruckle, the young girl who married Arthur in 1890, when he was twenty. The family history says that she was sixteen when she was married, but some documentation I have uncovered in Minnesota suggests that she was only fourteen. She came to Algernon with her father John and her sister Ida when she was about ten. The Luthers had already been here for two years, on a farm a few miles away from where John settled with his two daughters. John Ruckle's wife had recently died in Iowa, where the Ruckles had paused for ten years between Minnesota and Nebraska. Ella must have known her mother, Irena Harriman, and known her well, even though she left her girls orphans at a tender age. Ella and Ida took their orphan training to heart: they would leave their own children orphans at an age so young that their children would hardly remember being mothered.

Arthur and Ella probably attended school together when they could be spared from chores on their farms. I know only one thing about their courtship, and that I can deduce from the fact that they were married in June and my father was born in November (which may explain how Ella's age came to be adjusted from fourteen to sixteen). Marriage under these circumstances was not at all unusual in the pioneering period. I have a computer program that provides a courtesy beep as a reminder whenever I put in a date for a first child which is not a socially safe distance from the marriage. Last year I put in a thousand persons from my research on the Luthers, most of whom were part of the pioneering experience. The computer sounded like a hurdy-gurdy. The programmer who coded that beep had more sense of propriety than reality. I doubt that the Luthers were exceptionally lusty, though. That was how it was for most people among the working class in the last century. The accepted principle nearly everywhere was that you did not marry until you had a modicum of financial security. The novels of Dickens are full of sentiments to this effect, for example. But what happens when true love embraces those who do not even glimpse a hope of financial independence on the horizon? The state of matrimony wants motivation, as Micawber might say. A lovin' somethin' in the oven, positioned by intention or accident, could move even the most reluctant parents to give their approval and to make the sacrifices needed to launch the new couple on a life of their own.

Arthur and Ella went to live with her father and help with his farm. For years Arthur had walked the hills of Algernon with his own father, noting the workable lands that were still unclaimed, planning for the time when Arthur would be twenty-one and could file his own claim. But new settlers kept flowing in, and Arthur's age could not be hurried. When Arthur was old enough to take his own homestead there were no more lands available in the area. So they decided to remain on John Ruckle's farm. There may have been other reasons for this as well, but, whatever they were, the decision to continue their life together on her father's homestead would prove fatal.

Dad was born on the Ruckle farm at the beginning of November 1890. In the month that he was born Nebraska was in political turmoil. The crops had failed, and farmers were blaming the railroads and Eastern money for robbing them of fair profit on their labor. The Populists, a newly formed party representing farm interests, fielded a large slate of county and state candidates in the elections that fall. Omer Madison Kem was their candidate for the U.S. House of Representatives from the central district of Nebraska. When word reached Custer County that Kem had been elected as the first Populist representative from the state, the town square in Broken Bow erupted with bonfires, parades, and wild celebrations. A few days later Ella gave birth to her first son, and, caught up in the excitement of political change, Arthur and Ella named their first child Omer Kem after the new celebrity. My father was not alone in this curious distinction. Throughout his life he continued to hear of other Omer Kems born in Nebraska's decade of Populism. Kem himself went on to serve three terms, until, disillusioned by the frustration of trying to persuade Eastern politicians to support the Populist/Socialist programs, he took his family farther west.

As farmers' hopes for Populist policies from the national government were turned to disappointment, so the fortunes of Arthur and Ella's family also took a turn for the worse. When Dad was eighteen months old, a brother was born. But the spring of 1892 brought troubles. First one of the household, and then another, was incapacitated by illness. Neighbors must have taken time from the hard demands of their own farms to look to the chores of the Ruckle farm and to tend the sick. Although the Ruckles never knew it by its proper name, the sickness which gripped the household was probably typhoid fever.

In my imagination I can see Arthur and Ella, he in a farmer's coarse shirt and baggy woolen pants, she in a long-sleeved smock. I can imagine their days of summer labor, the young couple's winter conviviality, the horses and cattle they tended, the wagon they drove. I cannot picture these things because I have seen them in person, of course, or even because I have seen a photograph of them in these contexts, or because I have read a description of them. I can imagine them in these contexts because I have seen others living like this, or have read about them. What I know of other pioneer families can be extrapolated to the Ruckles and Luthers. The fact that they were just people, salt of the earth, having lives of neither high distinction or low notoriety, makes this picture in my head a credible one. The lives of the unchronicled masses are not unknown lives. They are, in fact, better known than those whose vectors took them on a tangential path from the social center. At the center, no verbal picture can compete with what we know from our own experience. On the periphery, no amount of explanation can make clear what cannot be understood. Thoreau, though he filled his journals with nearly two million words, left us puzzled by one night in the Concord jail.

Allow me the liberty, then, of encountering young Arthur and Ella through the gruesome expediency of a medical textbook. I want to know them so badly that I will take what help I can get. It is sometimes embarrassing, I realize, to visit people on the bed of sickness. Medical people must do this, of course, and the social codes are written to allow necessity the space to act. But normal interpersonal conventions break down in the face of physical suffering. I knew a woman who became severely ill. She sent a note to her social circles asking them not to come by. It seems that we do not easily expose our suffering. Even animals will crawl away to die.

The same social conventions say that "family is allowed," however. With this license I turned to the stacks of a medical library in search of typhoid. A library was more useful to me than talking to a North American physician: typhoid is unusual these days. Its propagation is highly dependent on the poor public health practiced in earlier centuries. Antibiotics have also lessened its terror.

In the library I found that there were three kinds of reference textbooks on disease. The older medical texts, written before 1890, are more likely to give case histories of single patients. In this century, up until World War II, the texts have fewer references to individual cases, and discuss the diseases with more confident generality. Modern texts, finally, are replete with references to the current literature, and tend to cite statistically significant findings from controlled studies of larger groups of patients. Of the three, I found that I preferred the middle level. Although older references were the most personal, the vocabulary in use today was not well developed then. Their descriptions lack the eye for events that even a lay person would exhibit today, and refer to a medical metaphysics which has a distinctly archaic feel. The newer texts are too impersonal. The professional medical vocabulary of the middle group, on the other hand, has become the lingua franca of a modern visit to the doctor's office. It might not be what doctors say to each other now, but it is the way their patients talk to them.

"Typho" in Greek was originally applied to something that smoldered, and gave off a cloud of smoke—a wick, for example. By extension, I suppose, the word was applied to those who were befuddled or bemused ("in a cloud"). It came to be applied to a set of diseases in which a prolonged high fever left the person in a state of mental confusion. It wasn't until the early years of the nineteenth century that typhoid fever was clearly distinguished from the endemic and less dangerous fevers carried about by human lice. These got the name (typhus fever), and the more deadly forms came to be called typhuslike, or typhoid.

The immediate cause of typhoid is a form of the common salmonella bacterium. It typically spreads from one host to another through water. The best approach to stopping its spread is to make sure that the water supply is not contaminated with fecal material from a typhoid carrier. Perhaps the reason that the whole Ruckle household contracted typhoid fever was because of a poor well which communicated in some deadly way with the septic arrangements on the farm. This doesn't explain how the germ found its way to the farm in the first place, however.

A possible source for some typhoid cases on the Great Plains in the last century was oysters. Today, except in coastal areas, oysters are food for the connoisseur. It was a puzzle to me how my father, who probably never ate more than home cooking or standard restaurant fare in his entire life, might have acquired a fondness for oysters. The puzzle was resolved a few years ago when I began to read about the early history of the Midwest. The Granges, formed by a farmers' movement which began in the 1870s, sometimes sponsored large community oyster suppers. Oysters were cheap in the last century. They became available when the railroads came through: oysters could be easily transported during the cooler months. And seafood coming from shallow tidewaters where sewage is directly discharged can be contaminated with typhoid bacteria.

It is not necessary to seek exotic sources, however, to explain typhoid's presence in Algernon. Twenty-five thousand people died of typhoid in the Civil War years, and as survivors of the disease moved west they brought typhoid with them. It has been shown that people can become passive carriers of the typhoid salmonella up to ten years after recovering from the disease. What carrier might have come to visit, or who Arthur or Ella or John Ruckle may have visited, we will never know. The short of it is that typhoid arrived at the Ruckle farm in the spring of 1892. When it departed at the end of the summer, it left behind an emaciated Arthur and his sickened son in the care of the Luthers, and fresh graves for the rest of the household here in Mason City.

Let us assume that Arthur's father-in-law contracted the typhoid infection first, since he was the first to die. The exact date of his death is not certain. I only know that he was dead by late spring. The sequence of dates can be reconstructed. Somewhere in, say, early March, soon after the thaw, typhoid bacilli entered John Ruckle's stomach. Ella, probably the principal housekeeper on her father's farm, had just given birth to a child, so the family's eating routine might well have been disrupted, perhaps giving rise to the occasion for the initial typhoid exposure. Within hours of ingesting the infected substance, the typhoid bacteria will have passed to Ruckle's bloodstream. Now a long incubation period begins, lasting from two to three weeks. In late March the disease begins to show. "The onset," Conybeare says in his medical textbook, "is insidious." In some cases "the patient may walk around for days while actually suffering from the disease." Soon Ruckle takes to bed with the first stage of the disease. The fever begins to climb, approaching 104 degrees by the end of the first week of overt illness. There is a headache, so severe that typhoid is sometimes mistaken for meningitis in the first week. Along with the headache comes giddiness, thirst, and pain in the arms and legs. His bowels stop moving, and his tongue is furry and dry.

This easy part is now past. Between Ruckle and his maker are ten days of living hell. When the second stage begins, the patient becomes stuporous. "Muttering delirium may be present, particularly at night." The abdomen swells, and the swollen spleen is detectable. Pink spots appear. He "sinks in to a 'typhoid state' characterized by extreme prostration." The cloud has descended, taking away the sense but not the sensation. The stuporous state of the daytime may turn into violent delirium at night, the patient "slipping down in the bed, plucking at the bedclothes, and groping for non-existent objects." He becomes incontinent. Constipation turns to pea-soup diarrhea. The contaminated bedcovers are highly infectious. Most physicians in hospitals treating typhoid patients end up with their own staff as patients. A bright flush appears on Ruckle's cheeks, and his eyes are sunken, pupils dilated. Hiccoughs aggravate the swollen abdomen.

Complications can set in. The typhoid patches on the bowels may perforate. Excrement enters the patient's abdomen, and fresh blood flows from the anus. If this happens the body becomes rigid, and begins to shake. In addition to the danger of perforation, reduced and weakened breathing can lead to lobar pneumonia. Should the patient recover, phlebitis (clots in the legs and arms) is a real danger. It is not uncommon, moreover, for the recuperating person to experience a variety of psychiatric disorders, ranging from dullness to schizophrenia. There may be more real complications from typhoid fever than from any comparable infection. "The whole illness," says Christie's text, "is one of the longest and most exhausting of all acute infections, and to anyone who has seen typhoid fever at its worst, the wonder is always that the patient has the power to recover from such a disease."

John Ruckle succumbs after two weeks of pain and delirium. For the next few weeks the small family must have been absorbed with matters relating to the loss of the head of the household. There will be a funeral, and the land Ruckle owned must be legally transferred to his children. The seasons do not pause for death: crops must be planted and weeded. For a few weeks the family may have thought that the rest had escaped the disease. The typhoid bacteria are not gone, however. For most of the summer they wait, dormant, in blood or water. In the height of the August heat they become active. Ruckle's daughters and their husbands and children now begin to show the early stages of the disease. By the end of September, only Arthur and his son are alive. Full recovery, I read, takes up to two months. The elections in November of 1892 must have held little interest to the weakened Arthur. As he took the first trembling steps in the cooling autumn air after a season of suffering and loss, the powers that be must have seemed utterly malign. Although he would remarry, and have another family of six children, he would never again name a child after a political figure.

Solomon
Butcher

From the cemetery I drive three miles west to the place where the Ruckle and Luther homesteads were situated. To find the two homestead properties I use a high-resolution county map on which I have marked the two quarter-section homesteads. The locations were derived from the section, township, and range numbers in the homestead records. This is often the only way to find these ancient farms. At least they can be found. Genealogists who work with the metes and bounds system in the eastern and southern United States face a major piece of detective work to find the vanished boundary markings. The exact location of the homestead lands associated with Arthur's father and John Ruckle has not been well preserved in the communal memory of their descendants. My father was probably the last living person who could have driven to the right spot without recourse to the grid lines of a plat map.

I'm not really expecting to find anything on the Luther homestead, so I am not disappointed as I top the last hill and begin to parallel the homestead land. It's just a piece of middling land, part pasture, part plowed and ready for planting. There is no house, or even a vestige of a house. A hundred years ago there would have been several dwellings in view from here, at least one family every quarter section. Today the average farm size is well over a square mile.

Arthur's family held this land for a mere five years. Perhaps a dozen other farmers have owned and sold it since. This real estate is only important to my pilgrimage for two reasons. One reason is a picture. The other reason is that, among the crowd of subsequent owners, the Luthers were the first.

"First owners" only has meaning within the larger fiction that the land was created fresh and unclaimed minutes before some American or European settler signed a document in a land claim office. County histories raise themselves to an almost religious mania when speaking of these first claimants. The first ones are The Pioneers, whether they stayed for five years or fifty. The county histories written around the turn of the century will list page after page of these claims. They are the Book of Numbers in the narrative of beginnings. I have been through many county courthouses looking at the early land records. In none of these have I ever seen an entry of ownership predating the land patents of the settlers. (Even some of the land patents themselves were included retroactively, since the patent record was originally at a land office rather than a courthouse. The property would not usually appear in the official county records until the patentee sold or mortgaged it.) In almost every case, however, the Indian claims to these same lands were extinguished by a process of *purchase.* If the Indians could sell it, they must have owned it. If they owned it, why is their transaction with the federal government not recorded for this piece of land?

What is to be noticed here is the peculiar usage of the word "ownership" in land records which allows it to be applied to the pioneers but not to the Indians. Ownership, however, is a turtle word, as in the story of the missionary who had engaged the local wise man in a debate about the origin of the world. On being told that the world was supported on the back of a great turtle, the missionary asked, smugly, "And what does the turtle stand on?" The sage replied, "A larger turtle." The missionary, sensing a reductio around the corner, continued "And what does that turtle stand on?" The wise man, thinking for only a brief moment, replied "It will do you no good, ma'am. It's turtles all the way down." The concept of ownership, like turtles, has no limit within itself. If it applies at all, it applies all the way down to the bottom. Someone owned the land as soon as there was someone there to own it who could fulfill the minimal conditions of ownership. Property, and the ownership of it, is one of those big, bounding, defining concepts which sets the horizons for discourse. We do not know how to change what such words mean without reworking sizable chunks of other parts of our language. When we use the word in a way that changes its meaning, we stand on the precipitous edge of ambiguity. So the Indians were, by all that language can discover, owners of this property.

But they are owners who are not in the official ownership records. It seems, then, that there are owners, and there are owners. Indians are one kind of owner, the homesteaders are another. Custom has the task of dividing what language unifies. To keep language from expressing itself requires a strong custom, firmly embedded in human nature and need. It calls for a turtle which can not only support all the turtles above it, but can stop foundational questions from being applied to itself. Even a custom as deeply entrenched as slavery was not able to hold language apart. The language of individual rights used in the revolutionary era contributed to the eventual emancipation of the slaves. Although the rights embodied in the U.S. Constitution were not originally extended to blacks under slavery, it did not explicitly exclude them. It could not have excluded them, or the high language of human rights would have been trivialized. And so the seeds of contradiction, cast into the soil of language, must either come up as hypocritical weeds or be rooted out. The Civil War was a mighty weeding of a badly overgrown semantic garden.

The same kind of semantic process gave rise to homesteading. As it was practiced between 1840 and 1880, homesteading was an attempt to resolve ambiguities in the concept of property which were planted when the Europeans began to force the Indians westward. It was a way to keep turtle ownership from going all the way down. The government could not continue to hold and sell the purchased lands itself without crediting the previous Indian ownership as one of the prerequisites of a valid sale. The federals redistributed Indian lands in two ways at first. One was to give them away as bounty lands to soldiers who had fought in U.S. wars. The other was to sell the lands in large chunks to quasi-corporate entities (railroads, land companies) who would resell them to settlers. As means to get a mass of settlers onto the properties and the lands under development, both devices turned out to be partial failures. Land companies continued to hold large parcels of land out of development. Soldiers sold their bounty certificates for immediate cash to large developers, who in turn held these or resold them at inflated prices. Both of these outcomes tended to undercut the basic thesis underlying the alienation of Indian lands: that the land was required to accommodate the pressing masses who needed new lands for homes and farms. Instead of a potent social movement which was able to divide the notion of ownership, all the government got was political legerdemain. A modern political analysis might have accused the government of *laundering* the lands. What was needed was some social use of the land which would allow ownership to have two domains of application, one before the settlers came, and one after. For a brief time the corporations and soldiers were convenient recipients: the corporations, because by their bankruptcies and rechartering the thread of ownership could not be traced through time, and the military, because soldiers could be construed to have justly received the land without a sale, in compensation for wars in which the Indians, with a perverse instinct, had almost unfailingly chosen the wrong side.

Such laundering, however, can only hide ambiguity, it cannot resolve it. For these reasons the government was moved, first in the Pre-emption Act of 1841, and later in the Homestead Act of 1862, to change the moral basis of land acquisition. Under the Homestead Act, persons who were heads of household were "entitled" to a 160-acre tract of western land, if only they would settle on it and improve it. Waves of pressing immigrations, coupled with the ideology of manifest destiny, provided the moral climate for the re-creation of the western lands. The lands were indeed purchased from the Indians, but they were then given away to meet the strong social pressures of living space. And so the chain of ownership was broken. One set of owners, the Indians, had held the land by natural possession and had given it up by sale, and the other set of owners now held the land by the entitlement of social urgency. Thus did the notions of homesteading and property come to live quietly under the same roof.

Or so the story goes. Perceptions of moral trends are always easier in long retrospect. I frankly doubt that Arthur's father ever gave these issues a second thought when he moved his family onto this freshly laundered land. Twelve children and no money in the bank does not provide the best context for sensitive historical analysis. But I have dropped down these hundred years so easily in the last hour that the Indian ghosts under this pioneer land do not seem so far away. I can sense them just below my feet. They are not ghosts that I would like to awaken.

The other reason I wanted to see this homestead was to match it against a picture. The picture is one of the thousands taken by the frontier photographer Solomon Butcher in Nebraska's pioneer era. Butcher ranged this county from one end to the other doing his version of Matthew Brady. The battlefields he photographed were the nearly invisible demarcations between the hopes of the settlers and the intractable climate of central Nebraska. Butcher probably didn't know that he was photographing a war. At first he was just trying to support his homesteading habit. He opened a photographic studio about thirty miles north of Algernon, near Sargent. In 1886 he conceived the idea of a photographic history of Custer County. Over the next seven years he managed to average nearly one Custer County photograph a day. Many of these have survived in the original large glass negatives.

The pictures are farm and family portraits. The first homes of hundreds of The Pioneers are on these plates. They are astonishingly clear in the fine detail. Though I had known the pictures for many years through Butcher's own books and through the prints and copies on file in historical societies, it was not until I saw the precise reproductions in John Carter's *Solomon Butcher: Photographing the American Dream* that I understood how attractive the first copies must have looked to those for whom he took the originals.

What makes Butcher's pictures unique is not their technical quality, though. It is the way he tells a minute piece of a larger story with each picture. The spirit of Butcher's interpretations is so far from what is considered to be the modern standard that it is difficult to apply the vocabulary of aesthetic criticism. In each exposure there is a compromise between what

Solomon Butcher's photograph of the Luthers in Mason City, 1888. Arthur is the boy stand-ing in the middle. Henry is seated, holding the picture. Elizabeth has the baby on her lap. Solomon D. Butcher Collection, Nebraska State Historical Society.

the families wanted and the part that the picture was playing in Butcher's vaster conception of frontier life. He was not above adding the silliest re-touchings to the plates, or posing his customers in ridiculous theatrical stances. The naiveté of these pictures, however, calls attention to the fact that the picture itself was, for Butcher, the eye through which the spirit passed. The spirit was that of the Nebraska pioneer, and the almost daily struggle to turn a strange and uncomfortable land into a landscape of farm homesteads. The conflict between the dynamic of the events and the flatness of the image is an abiding tension in most of Butcher's photographs. These photographs are chapters in the story of the rise and fall of the pioneers' hope. Here is a family standing around the prairie grave of a dead child. Next to another

Detail: The woman standing in the doorway of the soddy is Mrs. Loyd, a neighbor. Her daughter is in a black frock with a corn stalk over her shoulder. Not pictured are Arthur's brothers James, Albert, and Jesse.

family is the team of horses which were daily partners in the effort to wrest the means of life from a grudging land. A field of withered and widely spaced corn crawls up to the front door of a soddy. Hogs slop in foot-deep mud a few paces in front of another opening in a sod wall. Family pictures are hauled out to be included in the portraits, sad testimony to the loneliness and isolation of the dry lands. The night before another of Butcher's photographs was taken a rain soaked the roof, and in the morning it collapsed, just minutes after a widower and his three children had gone outside.

In the Custer County photographs of the 1880s the sod house predominates. Butcher was fascinated by the role of the soddy in the life of the Great Plains settlers, and later in his life wrote a tract on the construction of these houses. The sod house resembles from a distance a house built of largish brick. On closer inspection the resemblance disappears, for the bricks are hairy three-inch-thick rectangles of sod, the only building material within the settlers' meager budgets. Like a log cabin in a forest, a sod house could be constructed on the prairie in only a day by a small crew of men and women. A glance at the backgrounds of Butcher's photographs shows a land almost totally devoid of trees. The absolutely necessary wood components—window sashes, doors, and ridgepole—were often carted in from long distances.

For being composed of only earth, the sod house was remarkably durable. Some partially sod houses were still in use when I was growing up in the 1950s. But the goal of the pioneer was to get out of the sod house as soon as possible. Its drawbacks are all too apparent. When it was dry, a fine dust sifted down continually. When it rained it was no better: sod roofs were known to drip on the inside for three days after a rain finished on the outside. There were, of course, advantages. But it was never a matter of economic calculation. People with aspirations simply did not continue to live in dirt homes. Its most obvious advantage—that anyone could build one for minimal cost—was its most evident disadvantage. Despite the fact that marvelously large and complex versions of the sod house were built, their days were numbered by the same factors that doomed the rough-hewn log house as a building technology for permanent homes. Sod houses are shelters in the same way that gruel is food.

In the spring of 1888 Solomon Butcher and his photography wagon passed through Algernon. Here he found the Luthers and the fourteen-year-old Arthur encamped on this quarter-section. Out of this encounter came a portrait of the family and their sod house. The picture has its complement of typical Butcher features: the central family ranged in front of the farmstead, less central persons (a visiting neighbor) in a further plane, the sod house, the teams of horses, the farm implements, and the heirlooms carried out to join the family circle. As though it were not enough to have the care of the nine children included in the picture, Arthur's father Henry holds a picture of another family group, perhaps the older children already married and out of the house.

Removing the picture from its folder, I hold it at arm's length. I had hoped, given the line of low hills on the margins of the photograph, to identify the place where the sod house stood, but there is a sameness to these rolling horizons that defeats my attempt to find Butcher's ancient perspective. Nor is it any use to examine the land. Sod houses had no foundations. A few years of plowing were enough to erase the evidence of a family's sojourn. An archaeologist turned loose here might be able to locate the house using a midden or the lining of the well. I remember as a child the small dumps with rusting stoves, parts of cars, and twisted barbed wire that marked the futile homesteads on each quarter-section of our ranch. But the ranch land had not been regularly (and should never have been) plowed. In this valley is enough rain, when the rains do not fail, to attract the plow. A hundred years of intermittent cropping have left me without a shrine. I slip my icon back in its case and leave the land to its spirits.

Saline County, Nebraska

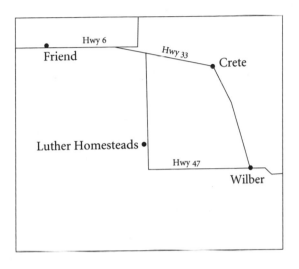

Dynasty

After a few minutes of tacking through square corners on gravel and dirt roads I am back on Highway 2. No need to look at the map for this. It would be impossible for anyone between here and the Allegheny Mountains to be lost for long, if only she had a compass or a good sense of direction. The secondary roads over most of this large midcontinent are straight, and follow section lines.

Directly behind me, past the line of rainfall, this dictum fails. The ranch where I grew up is at the nearer edge of the Nebraska Sandhills, one of the most unpopulated areas in the contiguous United States. Roads in this region are where you find them. There are stories no older than I am about people who lost their bearing in the Sandhills, and ended up wandering in large circles until overcome by exposure or thirst. Butcher, in his history of Custer County, also tells a story about this from the pioneer days. What gives coinage to these stories is, I think, an odd sensation which most people have felt as a child, but few as adults. It is the feeling of looking around and not wanting to be where you are, but not knowing which way to go to get where you want to be. It is the child whose hand slips away from the protective custody of the parent in a large store. It is the occasional sailor who has always trimmed within line-of-sight of some shore until he is one day caught in a heavy fog at a distance too great to hear the sounds of land. It is the sense of utter abandonment. The uniqueness of the sensation suggests that it should have its own word. Let us call it *coup d'horizon.*

A few times the Sandhills have pulled this trick on me. I would be out walking and suddenly realize that I did not know which way I was going. The wind-shaped hills at every box of the compass would reach in to confront me like the walls of a large prison, one section of sand ridges as like to the other as two waves on the sea. Coup d'horizon grabs you in the gut first, so it is a subtype of panic. But it moves quickly to the head. A lightness, almost a dizziness, pervades the region above the ears. The sensation of confinement reverses during its upward flow. Your eyes try to focus on the horizon, but the land seems like a vast rubber sheet that is being stretched to the points of infinity in every direction. The sky begins a tugging match with the earth to pull you apart at the neck. You have a sudden desire to be as near to the ground as possible. People have been known to start crawling. The stereotype of the thirsting man scrabbling at the desert sand may have its origin from some storyteller's memory of a coup d'horizon event. Travelers in vast deserts must know this feeling intimately. And when do sailors who leave the sight of land stop being seized by this sensation an hour out of every port?

The whole experience is unpleasant in the extreme. Many of the first settlers in this region who kept journals have described it. The trapper Jim Bridger, when asked if he had ever been lost, is supposed to have replied "No, but for several weeks I didn't know where I was." Trapper Jim was not contradicting himself. He knew where he was in terms of map features. It was coup d'horizon he was remembering. Civilization had let go of his hand.

The day has begun to warm up. The next stop is over two hours away. My safety line of ancestors is there where I can reach it, though, so I can let my attention relax for a while. I set the cruise control and begin the next leg, from Mason City to Grand Island, moving southeast. Grand Island, one of the towns blessed with the interstate, is still an hour away. The scenery that begins to roll by is mostly river valley topography, though there is no real river here, just creeks paralleling, then moving off to join one of the three Loup rivers to the north and south of my line of travel. The country around here has sections that are pure Sandhills, but these are leprous spots on a gentler terrain which does not, for the most part, show the shaping of the wind in its land forms. I have always been perplexed how the map makers have been able to draw a line that shows exactly where the Sandhills begin. For some years I fancied that it was on the very land that was my family's ranch west of Broken Bow, since the soil on our land moved from a richer, subirrigated sandy loam to pure Sandhills sand when you traveled across it from east to west. I realize now that this can happen anywhere this side of Grand Island. Even up in the middle of the desolate Sandhills region there are fertile arteries along the streams. And here, five miles in any direction, pockets of Sandhills can trap the moving car. These topographic moves are all analog transitions overlaid with the digital delineations of a cartographer. "Sandhills" means nothing in an inch-by-inch analysis. Even the edge of a lake, so clear on a map, fractals down to micrometer meaninglessness when looked at too closely. The same analog/digital conflict holds for ideas as well. Since leaving Mason City I have crossed the borders of a thousand concepts. Exactly when I crossed any particular margin, however, was known only at the level of discourse to which the concept belonged, and only if the border itself was not examined too closely. Look too hard at a concept and its horizons slip away into an infinity of meaning and countermeaning. You can find yourself frozen in conceptual space by a semantic version of coup d'horizon. Wrestling with a word like "ownership" can leave you sitting in the nursery chanting rhymes and nonsense songs. Words are living creatures which do not bear too much dissection without collapsing into mortified contradictions.

The first real change in the landscape happens as I move into the broad Platte valley. I missed the transition. But I have watched for it before, with all my attention, and still couldn't catch it. Instead of hills around me, I now see a flat stretch of land in three directions, so wide that I can't see the hills on the other side. If this were my first trip, I might think I had entered an immense plain. It is this valley, I have always assumed, that gives Nebraska its reputation for being flat. The westward interstate, following the Oregon Trail for long stretches, tracks down the Platte valley for most of the length of the state. Unless you are perceptive, and notice the hills rising to the north or the south whenever the interstate wanders from the valley center, you would think that the whole state was like this valley. When people find out that I am from Nebraska they often comment on the experience of driving through the state to points west: "I thought the state would never end! We started in Nebraska in the morning, and by the time we stopped we weren't out of it. It was as flat and featureless as a pancake." It does not occur to them that they might have been driving up a long fairway too wide to show the roughs.

The first Europeans who came through also used this river valley. The earliest groups were just passing through, heading west for furs and gold. They welcomed the wide chute, since it gave them a chance to see hostile bands of Indians as they approached. It was a corridor through which the U.S. Cavalry could, by skirmish and treaty (used indifferently), secure safe passage for the moving trains of wagons. This is, I assume, the reason that the ancient trails, and the modern roads following them, pass as nearly down the center as the meandering Platte River allows. Nebraska was boring for the ones heading on west, to judge by their journals. Some of the first settlers also noted this effect. Willa Cather writes of coming to Nebraska as a young girl: "The only thing very noticeable about Nebraska was that it was still, all day long, Nebraska." She is one of the few locals who made it big without the aid of television or movies. She wrote most of her books after she left Nebraska.

I read, years ago, that Nebraska has one of the most extensive drainage systems in the United States. There are more miles of rivers and creeks here than in almost any other place. You would expect some kind of Eden, but the subtext is that the rivers and streams carry the water *away*. And for long stretches of the year hardly any water flows through the creek beds. Probably no land on earth is better watered to less effect than this. The Platte, which I am now approaching, is, according to the local adage, "a mile wide and an inch deep," but today the water volumes of spring will make it look like any of the other strong, deep rivers further east. Before crossing the sand beds of the Platte system I skirt the edge of Grand Island. Soon I am on Interstate 80, heading eastward, toward Lincoln. I won't make Lincoln today: another station will interrupt the pilgrimage in about an hour.

This is partly a collecting expedition. There is nothing about a pilgrimage that contradicts the urge to bring back souvenirs. The typical pilgrimage in the Middle Ages was also a time for collecting. The shrines were surrounded by vendors of relics and other memorabilia of the sacred place. Pilgrims to Canterbury would buy a token and wear it proudly for the rest of their lives as an emblem of the pilgrimage. The knight who went to the Holy Land would return burdened with items of local color from the places through which he passed. So I will be a pilgrim, but I will also collect.

Those who do genealogical work collect ancestors just as bird watchers collect bird sightings. Bird-watching is supposed to be the single most common hobby in North America. For how many millions is there a thrill in being able to add just one more check to a life list? I believe, however, that genealogy may be a more common (if less healthy) hobby than bird-watching. Genealogical hobbyists collect dead ancestors with a fervor that makes some bird watchers seem downright lackadaisical. We have our own life lists. They are pedigree charts with four grandparents, eight great-grandparents, sixteen great-great-grandparents, and on up. At each level are boxes waiting to be filled with names, dates, and places. A count of my life list shows that there are now thirty-two names from my great-grandparents on up (Most people know about their parents and grandparents without a lot of research. Most bird-watchers get robins, blackbirds, and sparrows by looking out the window.) Of these thirty-two upper-level ancestors, the names of nine were available to me from others in my immediate family. So twenty-three of them I have collected on trips like this. That is nothing, however: some genealogists have collected hundreds. So, although this pilgrimage is not just about collecting, I won't complain if I pick up the occasional sighting. Bird-watchers have been known to swing their cars to the side of the road and tear off across fields of briar and cocklebur on the chance of single bird. My friends know to indulge my passion for visiting courthouses and genealogical libraries on cross-county trips, even if they can't understand it. The problems and pleasures of collecting are arcane to the point of invisibility to those who do not share the obsession.

Ancestor collecting can be done carelessly, or it can be done with sensitivity and finesse. It is hard to explain to someone who does not know our art, for example, why we count one set of circumstances as a nearly certain indication of a sought relationship, and at the same time discount another set. You learn to smell connections where they can't be seen. You feel your way through a maze of documents, learning to palpate the legal jargon of wills for the tumors under the skin, tracing the edges of family secrets with your probing. Discrepancies in dates come to you like out-of-balance statements to auditors. Social relationships are followed detective-like down the tracks of lodge memberships, land transfers, and probate records. Some of this is an innate skill, but the full sensitivities are acquired through long exposure, catalyzed, I am told, by an enzyme found in the dung of mites who feed exclusively on the dust from century-old ledgers.

And there are ceremonies, enough to delight the loftiest high-church mind. Heraldry, though not my cup of tea, is still part of the hobby, and peerage is one of genealogy's parents. But the act of collecting is itself the subject of socialized habit. Genealogists tend to own postage scales, for example. They know well the ritual of going into post offices and, to the dismay of the clerks, trying to buy international postage coupons. The wait for the morning mail is a complete ceremony in itself, and the subject of much in-group humor. Persons who do genealogy must learn forms of speech used with employees in the courthouses and record offices. Everything they do gets written down, and ends up in three-ring binders or manila folders. Charts are drawn to the standard forms of record plan, family group, pedigree, and Ahnentafel. Middle names are never skipped. They know how names get transformed into nicknames, converse fluently about the child-naming patterns of the various immigrant groups, and keep soft-lead pencils and blank paper in the car for tracing gravestones. They can load ten different kinds of microfilm readers faster than a projectionist can thread a projector.

This trip is not, however, a genealogical collecting trip, any more than a pilgrimage is a sightseeing tour. But I can't help collecting, and the tools I will use to get along are the tools I have learned as a part of the hobby, so it may be mere quibbling to try to separate the means and ends in actual practice. At the conceptual level, though, the distinctions matter. At all costs, the mind of the pilgrim must be maintained through the dust and the trials of the pilgrimage itself. Trinkets are one thing, self-understanding is another.

It is time to move along the rope to the next stake in my safety line. In Mason City I was looking for my grandfather Arthur. There I had hardly crossed the edges of living memory. At the next stop I will visit the family in which Arthur was raised. This is the family that was displayed in the Butcher photograph. The father in this family was *Henry Luther*, the mother was *Elizabeth Cline*. These names, before we have finished with them, will take us across half of the United States.

I did not know either of them. They were gone many years before I came on the scene. They are known more in caricature than as real and intimate persons, even to many of my aunts and uncles. Henry and Elizabeth have the privilege of being patriarch and matriarch of a line of descent in the narratives of family history. I don't fully understand how such designations get bestowed in the otherwise seamless flow of generations. The special treatment of a single generation as the source of a family line goes against intuition: you would think that any pair could be treated as the head of a line. This is not how it happens, however. One couple becomes a nodal point, a thick subtrunk of the family tree which supports all of the subsequent ramification. Nor is this an artifice of the genealogist. In this respect the genealogist is a servant of the oral tradition of families they are researching. I call this effect *dynasty*. As the word is traditionally used, dynastic status among royalty is changed when there is a major shift from a direct line of descent. This is not what I mean by it here, since no shift of bloodlines is involved. What I am talking about is the effect produced when one couple comes to be considered at once the culmination of previous and less visible lines of descent, and at the same time the head of a renewed line.

One way to achieve this effect is to have a lot of children. This may be how

Henry and Elizabeth mounted the dynastic ladder. Of Elizabeth's fourteen live births, eleven went on to have families of their own, and several of the children's families were also large. In the current family history 1,300 of their descendants have been chronicled, and many hundreds of others have not made it into the preserved records. But there are dynastic heads who had small families, so this can't be the full explanation. Status and wealth also seem to matter. It is as though the constant reference to these persons in the years of their influence ("It's all right, I'm the nephew of So-and-so.") prepares them for later canonization. I think we can rule this out in Henry's case, but I have seen this effect in other lines. It also seems to matter that the person or couple were responsible for moving the family away from the family home. Any immigrant to the United States, no matter how insignificant in wealth or status, or how few children, is automatically a candidate for dynastic head. The westward push across the Midwest in the last century was responsible for a great genealogical reshaping of family trees. This factor comes into play in the case of Henry and Elizabeth Luther. They made their ancestors disappear by transferring a new family through several states in less than forty years. It was a sleight of hand that left them at the top of the family totem. Of their thousand or so descendants, only a handful have any chance at being considered for dynastic status in their own right.

The place I am looking for is in Saline County, about thirty miles southwest of Lincoln, Nebraska. Oral tradition refers to the towns of Friend and Wilber, but I have since learned that these were two distant, and equidistant, post offices. The place of interest is a farm between the two towns. It was the place where Henry and Elizabeth stayed the longest—fourteen years—on their way to central Nebraska. For the majority of their children, it was their native home. They say that the place where a child is living when she is ten is most likely to become the place she will say that she is "from." Some kind of domestic imprinting happens about that age which turns earlier and later homes into transient locations. Henry and Elizabeth left Saline County when half of their children were over ten. The move effectively divided the large family into two subfamilies. My grandfather was in the first half of the family. Though he was born in Kansas, and left Saline County when he was fourteen, Saline, wherever he lived and moved after that, was always the place he was from.

I will start from the town of Wilber, since that is the county seat and the location of the records I hope to find. As I leave the interstate and head south, I see that I will arrive on the lunch hour. No point in heading to the courthouse right away. In these small towns there is often a single person who can help you, and they take their lunch hours seriously. I grab a sandwich in one of the town cafés. I can feel the stares of the local people, but they are careful and I'm not offended. This town is off the main road. Real strangers are as rare as hens' teeth. If I stayed here more than a day someone in town—a waitress, the motel owner, the librarian—would make it his or her business to know my business, and the tale of it would spread within hours through the unofficial security network. No need to take offense: it's just the way it works. After telephones were installed in the farm area where I was reared, every hitchhiker was traced through the community by a cascade of phone messages. Before that it was a series of child runners flying over the back pastures. But the rule now seems to be that everyone gets a day's grace if they want it. Since I'll be gone tomorrow, I don't respond to the friendly eye contacts in a way that would lead to the conversation they would eventually require of strangers like me.

Saline

After a quick stop at the library in Wilber to look over what has been collected on local history and genealogy, I'm off to the courthouse. To my surprise the Saline courthouse is hard to find. I almost never have to ask about courthouses in the Midwest. Generally you can see them from anywhere in town; they are usually within a block or two of the town center. This one, however, is at the edge of town. As I round the corner and the building comes into view, I see that its style is about as bad and as good as I might have predicted.

Surely someone from another culture who had acquired a sensitivity for the integration of language and meaning in architectural statement would be struck speechless at these courthouses. They are so focal in their respective cityscapes, and so out of step with other buildings in the same towns. Yet the Midwest is dotted with thousands of them. A thousand of anything spread out over a million square miles and built in a space of eighty years would constitute some kind of aesthetic movement, one would think, and would merit at least a chapter in a book on American architecture; it is almost impossible, however, to find a single line on them as a group. The construction of these courthouses belongs to a dark period of U.S. architecture between the pure goals of the Jeffersonian Greek revival and the wash of modern styles after Sullivan. Architectural tastes in this period give rise to phrases such as "bombastic eclecticism" and "aesthetic chaos."

When the Midwestern counties were established, the first order of the day was to get up a public building that would convey a sense of official authority to a frontier community, and to provide a statement of the region's intention to move rapidly to the condition of a fully developed society. The edifice would have to shout the emphatic message that it was an outlying branch of the civilization of Europe and the Eastern states. There was no thought given to putting up a building with local materials in a local style. On the contrary, a courthouse had to be full of marble, high art, and polished brass. For real estate speculators to sell town lots, the county government structures had to provide a sense of an impending city. Midwestern town boosting, with all of its modern offshoots, began here.

If the need for architectural statement was not enough to demand a stone version of Eastern prestige, the press of time added its mandate. To be selected as the county seat was an imprimatur that guaranteed the success of a town. Huge battles were waged for the permanent siting of the county seat. Saline County was the location of one such dispute. The lands were filling up with all haste, and the fickle interlacing of transportation routes could alter the early perceptions of where a county seat (or even a state capitol) belonged. For the first twenty years after the fortunate towns were selected, they were in constant danger of losing a plebiscite and having the favor removed. One of the best ways to nail down the designation was to get up an expensive and impressive building whose possibility of being converted to another function was minimal. The solution to this was a county courthouse designed by reputable architects and built by imported engineers and craftsmen. The trick didn't always work. I remember seeing in southern Iowa a decaying courthouse standing alone in a farmer's field. Above the door, carved in stone were the words "County Court House." Some day I will stop to find the story behind that parliament of cows.

A prime piece of this process of town boosting sits here in Saline on its commodious square, set off by the early spring greening of its carefully tended lawns. An architectural firm must have pulled its plan right off the shelf. They typically took some standard plan for a public building in a New England or European site, redrew it on a small knoll with a prairie horizon, added the county name in Latin block characters above the lintel, and shipped it, a draftsman, and their best salesman off by rail and coach to meet with the gullible city commissioners. A few changes to satisfy the small need for uniqueness, a new draft with a convincing local landscape and horizon, and the plans were set. There was little haggling, I suspect. The county was buying prestige.

These buildings are such mixtures of Greek plain style and Gothic excrescence that the result is naive, like a Butcher photograph. You look at it and right through it. Nothing about the facade arrests the sense of aesthetic wonder. What you see when you look at these buildings is, plainly and simply, a social role. This building speaks government, and such authority as can be mustered for an anarchic people. It is the house of remembering and the throne of justice, the church of a classless democracy. As the church in New England raised its emblematic spire above the countryside, so these courthouses perdure as pure symbol on the squares of a thousand towns in the Midwest. The religion brought by the settlers made no objection, since it was largely a religious practice that had already turned away from forms of ecclesiastical authority and the trappings of civil government. The civic functions were easily transferred to the new shrines of democracy. At one time the churches had maintained the records of birth, death, and marriage. Now the keeper was the county government. Its magistrates wore the robes of priests, and its acolytes moved quietly through the high vaulted stone, bearing in one direction the writ of authority and in the other direction the petitions of the people to the altars of judgment. In the Christian tradition, however, to be wholly church is not to be fully government, so the borrowed symbols of Christianity were transformed by being merged with a pre-Christian element lifted from the civil religions of Greece and Rome. The consciousness of the Roman imperial tradition and Greek public life are as important here as the suffused ecclesiastical motifs: the church is also a pagan temple. It has icons of the emperor and the shapes of the gods in plaster and oil. A favorite euphemism in the last century for a courthouse was a "temple of justice."

I marvel at the nineteenth-century mind for whom these tiers of symbols stood in dynamic union. For me they fly apart with irresistible force. At the doorways of these church/temples I have to choose my symbol set. This particular courthouse has more of a Greek feeling, so the Christian symbolism fades into the background, and I enter the temple in a classical mode.

I am here to consult the oracle. For this the skill to divine the entrails of animals is needed. To the untrained eye they are just so many bowels and organs. To the diviner they hold the word of prophecy. I will ask these ledger books to tell me about Henry's family, and to see where I might be traveling this week. Whether there are other secrets to be told here, about myself and my own petitioner's heart, I do not know—I'll only know when I am further along. For now the utterances of the oracle are enough. Their meaning can wait.

The first step is to work through the indexes to these records. The volumes in these offices are thoroughly indexed. What the genealogical researcher has to learn, however, is that they are not indexed with family history in mind. They are indexed for the recondite legalities that occupy governments and courts. With land records, for example, the county does not usually care about finding all of the land you might have owned in the past. It does want to know, however, what the succession of ownership is for a given piece of land, so its title can be cleared. The genealogist, on the other hand, does not always care about what progression of persons might have held title to a farm, but she does care how many different properties were in the possession of the person being studied. When the clerks have to retrieve a birth certificate, they are usually doing it for a person who was born in the county. Birth records are therefore indexed by the name of the child. Researchers working on families, however, often want to know all of the children a woman—who may have had more than one last name—gave birth to, so the index can be clumsy to use. The result of all this is that the indexes, supposedly a door to the records themselves, are often the target of the search they were supposed to preclude. Genealogical societies spend a lot of time preparing indexes tailored to the person collecting ancestors.

Indexing is one of those social habits that define the self-consciousness of a people. It is a summary of values, a precis of truth. To understand indexing is to perceive the interplay of two contradictory forces. One force is our need to have easy *access* to a data set. The other force is the *energy* we must expend to organize the data and build our indexes. To construct an index we must eject a lot of information in order to gain a little access. One way to get a handle on indexes and the interaction of these forces is to think about how a map works. A map is not the same as the thing mapped. It would be most inconvenient if, in order to find my way across this state, I had to carry the entire state's highway system in the car's glove compartment. So what I carry is a reduction of the system of highways. A map is allowed to lose inessential information, details that may not be needed by the person using the map. A tiny square on a colored line is not a highway interchange, but it is enough to tell me, when I learn to scry the map, where an interchange is located. My overall understanding of how interchanges work, the map maker trusts, will lead me through the missing details. Drawing up such maps, and getting the images right, requires a lot of energy. In general, the more energy we expend to assemble good images, and the more images we assemble, the easier it is to use them to access what we have imaged.

In the dimension of time, the two forces of energy and access come into their most obvious opposition. These courthouses were faced with the question of whether they should spend a hundred person-hours a year to maintain an index that might cut the search time tenfold, from one hour to, for example, six minutes. Purely in terms of time-on-task, the answer to the indexing question for such an example would be that when you average 112 or more searches a year, you are better off taking the extra time to do the index. This, of course, is an example that is far too simplistic. A lot of the payoff comes in later years, when the number of records has increased. There are also other issues to be considered: matters of security, the complex way indexes can aid a variety of tasks, the likelihood of error, and so on. But somehow we are able to weigh these complex factors and to make the decision to index or not to index. The indexing in courthouse records represents settled social judgments that have been made about the interplay of energy and access in county record systems. Few genealogists would want to be without them. But we use them warily, realizing that we are adapting the tool to a foreign task. When the distrust and frustration get too high, we reorganize, cancel our next engagement, and go directly to the records themselves.

In a larger sense the data on Henry Luther's family in this courthouse are itself an index: it is not his life, just the extracted data about his life which have been collected in these records. These bits of data are an index to him because they point to him. Although the purpose of such meta-indexing takes us into the legal, judicial, and administrative consciousness of a nation, the indexing dynamics of energy and access still apply. Since the whole of a person's life cannot be put here, the issue faced by a society is what parts of an individual's life need to be indexed by a record system. The resolution of the issue is achieved by asking how often, and for what reasons, the person needs to be accessed. What all of these records represent are ways of finding Henry Luther in one of his social roles. Here is a land record where Henry bought some land: why is it here? It is here because we may have a legal need to find Henry in his role as owner of the land. Here is a marriage record for one of his children: why is it here? The answer, again, is that the court might have to find Henry's child as a spouse or father of legitimate children in an intestate probate. But did he love those children, or cherish his spouse? Was Henry a faithful tiller and keeper of the land he owned? The direct answer is not here, because the minimal social apparatus in place in the 1880s did not need to find Henry in that role. It was too much energy to expend for too little access.

What I have to face is that if I knew these records intimately, if it were possible to memorize them all, and trace all of the subtle relationships, I would still be guessing about most of things I want to ask Henry. The man that is here is a shadow, an index, to the flesh and spirit. This is Plato's cave. I trudge from one room of ledger books to another, pulling at the ankle irons. I squint over my shoulder at the vague images in the blinding light, but there is no world of forms out there for me to consult when the index images fail to convey their message. They have passed from the earth. I am at the mercy of the purposes of government as another generation perceived them.

Here, 120 years deep, and 200 miles from the starting point, there are still plenty of records to be found. Something turns up on Henry in all of the major document source areas. There are land records, marriage records, one probate record, and—what luck!—some school records. In more than one courthouse my inquiries about certain records have been met with the response "Sorry, lost in the fire." An incredibly large number of courthouses have been damaged and destroyed by fire. Even the federal government is not immune to the appetite of fire. The 1890 federal census was almost totally lost, for example. Here in Saline County there was no fire. The records are all in good shape. They are also open to the researcher. Within about fifty years this county will be hit by masses of genealogists; judging by the experience of older counties in Ohio and east, amateurs' access to the records will become more formally controlled. In this part of the country the clerks and professional title searchers working through these records still far outnumber the genealogists. One is aware of interest and politeness on the part of the staff. This far west they don't see all that many genealogical researchers. A friend of mine who was writing a dissertation at the University of Chicago was given a letter to a library in Pennsylvania which would allow him to consult part of their collection of nineteenth-century documents. When he finally got the documents from the librarian he couldn't find a place at any of the research tables to do his work. They were occupied by people tracing their genealogies. It is easy to understand why so many historians regard us with suspicion. Just as sensitive environments sometimes have to be restricted from the marauding hordes of bird watchers, these irreplaceable documents must eventually be guarded from the masses of ancestor collectors. To be fair I should point out that genealogical societies are usually at the forefront in the preservation and publication of the endangered county records. But there are so many of us, and it takes so long to train searchers how to respect the value of what they handle, that we would be unrealistic to expect eternal openness.

Like a Polaroid snapshot, an outline image of Henry emerges from the records. Henry and Elizabeth came here in 1871 with Henry's mother and three of Henry's sisters. A brother followed soon after. They acquired land by patent at a land office, so they were the first legal owners of the individual parcels. The whole county went from a few hundred settlers to a fully occupied land in the space of about five years. By 1875 there were one or two homesteads, with their associated soddies and cabins, on every quarter section. A rough calculation suggests that the farming population alone would account for 1,500 families in Saline County. Add to this the support population in the towns and we see that well over 10,000 souls came to camp in this county in just a few years. Among them were Henry and Elizabeth and the first half of their family. Arthur was only a year old. Henry, two of Henry's sisters, and his mother each took neighboring eighty-acre farms. The contiguous parcels made up a half-section. Within a few years one sister would die, and her four children would be scattered among the relatives. Her children are poorly represented in the school records. Education is a luxury when the family unit is not intact. After a few more deaths in the family, and the marriage of the oldest of his children, Henry left Saline. None of his siblings went with him. It was this last break, after Henry's family had become large and self-contained, that was the finishing touch in the picture of Henry and Elizabeth as heads of a new dynastic line.

You do not know what the oracle will say when you enter these temples. On some days the oracle is talkative and practical, nearly comfortable. On some days the oracle is fey and long-sighted. Today has been a little of both: although there are lots of good records on the family, there is nothing that clearly shows what I might find or do in the days ahead. But it is the nature of oracle to be enigmatic, so there may be a level in this discourse that is past my understanding. I write it all down, just in case.

Roll of
the Dice

From the courthouse it's a ten-mile drive to Henry and Elizabeth's home-stead site. To find the land I make use of the township/section/range loca-tors again. The sun is setting as I finally triangulate on the homestead site by using section line roads and the car odometer. This land, I find, is also devoid of houses. A drive around the properties suggests no obvious place where the farmsteads might have stood. One suspects that the houses them-selves, such as they were, may have been clumped together, even though Henry, his mother, and two sisters each owned four distinct eighty-acre homesteads.

The differences between this land and the farms in Custer County is subtle but significant. As I look out over the land in the fading light I can see that there is very little pasture. It is almost all put to crops. Nor do I see any evidence of irrigation systems. This land gets a few more inches of annual rainfall than the Custer County land. It still has the tree-barren prairie look, but this is farmable prairie. The soil is less sandy. The loam runs deep. This is, as the phrase goes, *good* land. Why, then, did Henry leave this? Why would anyone who knew how to farm leave such land to gamble on the rains further west? But competent farmers did leave here, in droves. At the time of first settlement the names were all English/Irish and German. Within twenty years most of this land would be in the hands of a second wave of settlers who were nearly all Czech. The graveyard just north of this land, which was established by the Luthers to hold the four or five members of the extended family who unwillingly made this their permanent home, is today full of stones with sibilant Czech surnames. The Czech graves are well tended. Those in them sleep in peace, for their descendants are still here to preserve their memories and graves. The graves from the first wave, however, are untended. Most of the their headstones are broken or missing. They are unremembered, either by their people or by the land.

If only Henry and Elizabeth, of all of these thousands of settlers, had left, the answer might be sought in the family dynamics. After all, children do break with parents, and brothers with sisters. When so many leave, however, the personal reasons won't stretch far enough to cover the social causes. Henry and Elizabeth and the other homesteaders must have left here because they didn't find what they were looking for. What, then, were they looking for? You don't have to read many recapitulations of the virtues of pioneer movement to pick up the impression that the dream of a self-sustaining, honest farm life was what brought our progenitors to these new lands. Those who write about the pioneers are careful to bracket the pioneer days between two less admirable eras. Before the pioneers were the trappers, buffalo hunters, miners, and ranchers, all of whom came to make a profit, to take the wealth of the land for their own avaricious ends. After the pioneer period comes the modern age, where land has become a commodity and farms are businesses whose business is farming, and land is valued only for its economic bottom line. In between these two greedy ages are the noble pioneers, who came for the integrity of home and hearth in a rural setting. They came, we are led to believe, to husband the land, gently to transform it from a wilderness into a place of quiet, fruitful habitation. Our current problems, such analysis suggests, stem from having abandoned the purity of the pioneers' quest.

Any contrast so stark should immediately be suspect. The records of the pioneer settlers, no matter what slant they and their biographers placed on their motives in a later day, suggest that they came to the land with economic goals. The push westward was the big land grab, the first great national lottery. They came for their slice of the public pie. For those whose place in life left them without opportunity for quick enrichment, the West was a place where they could have the chance to make it. To stay in the East was to have to work thirty years for the chance, if the weather held and crops produced, to have a minimal farmstead which was free and clear. Here in the homestead lands the time was shortened to five years.

There were, of course, countervailing conditions. Most who came did not get wealthy, just as most of those who went to California for gold found only sickness, poverty, or death. Few actually made it pay. These settlers knew that the odds were not necessarily stacked in their favor. What the gambler has to see is not a sure thing, however; all that is needed to engage his attention is a reasonable chance to succeed. It was this light in the eyes of the pioneers, as much as it was the vision of home and hearth, that brought them out of the East, and caused them, generation by generation, to follow the promise of prosperity into the wilderness. They crowded in, staked by the government, for their chance at the gaming table.

Henry came for wealth, and he left, I fear, when the promise of that success had dimmed, and the opportunity came to spin the wheel again in Custer County. By the time he left he had, moreover, four sons on the edge of adulthood who would have wanted their turn at the table. How could he criticize their desire? He had followed his own lust for success, and had given his children the genetic and social bent to risk life for wealth.

One of the great tragedies of the rush for land and wealth was that the same forces that had constricted opportunities in the East followed hard after those who moved west. The deck was no less stacked against them here than it was back there. It is ironic that they left. Hindsight tells us that the ones who stayed behind had the best chance of economic success. It was, however, a slow success, measured over generations, and not the sort of adventure which could engage the imagination of those willing to risk a little for a lot. Revisionist interpretations of the pioneer experience have been appearing in recent years. Schlissel, Gibbens, and Hampsten, in their survey *Far From Home: Families of the Westward Journey*, tell how the promise of wealth became the mechanism for the sufferings and displacement of three typical pioneering families. Their stories, with a few changes, might stand for Henry's.

The means used to defeat the economic hopes of the settlers in this part of the Midwest was the mortgage. Under the homestead acts the land was cheap. A quarter-section could be had for 200 dollars or less. It was not unusual for the same land to be valued at 1,000 dollars only a few years later. The Eastern entrepreneurs organized large mortgage companies whose representatives were there with the needed cash as soon as the settler had legal title. For someone who had submitted to a journey of so many miles and years of hand-to-mouth hardship to attain the goal of land ownership, the prospect of a thriving, productive farm seemed to be an outcome so certain that the risk represented by the mortgage was hardly to be considered. It was, moreover, the only way that the project of homesteading could be brought to its fulfillment, the only way that a real house could be constructed, the only way that the debts of the years of deprivation could be repaid, and that the family could have proper clothing and a few of the amenities of civilization. And it was, sad to say, the only way the farmer could be staked for the next round of gambling.

For the next round the payoff was smaller and the risks were greater. But the homesteader was hooked. The alternative was to sell out, move back East without enough money to buy the necessary land, and submit humbly to the system which he had criticized in the first place. The few hundred dollars that would be left after debts were paid and the farm was sold would be hardly more than the homesteader had started with at the beginning of the process. By this time there was a growing family whose best chance for success seemed to lie with a farm enterprise. Taking on a mortgage was about as inevitable as the cold of the prairie winter. And about as lethal. The usurious rates—often in excess of ten percent, at a time of practically no inflation—meant that there had to be a cash excess each year on the premium due date. The only way to generate that excess was to sell farm produce. But sell to whom? Most of their neighbors were farmers, and had little need for the produce nor the ability to pay cash for what they did require. The scanty needs of the nonfarming support population were satisfied by gardens and Saturday markets. The product had to be sold back East. But sales to the East meant that goods had to be transported, and the new rail system was the only way to get it there. The rail system, however, was in a phase of costly expansion, and the rates charged for the shipment of grain and animals was at times more than what the farmer could get for his crop in the Eastern markets.

There are still stories around today about the impact of mortgage day on the farm family. It often meant the sale of a favorite animal, or the loss of some previously essential item, such as a buggy or a piece of furniture. It was the injustice of the mortgage system which focused farmers' dissent during the Populist movements of the 1880s and 1890s. At mass rallies farmers would bring their mortgage papers and wave them in the air, as if to say "this paper is all that stands between me and defeat." That paper, however, might as well have been a chain of iron. The farmers were in the grip of the same system that had enslaved them in the East. The only difference had been the few years at the table, when there was at least a feeling that they could have been free. Now the game was over. A few had won, most had lost, and by the early twentieth century life settled down to its old expectations in the newly settled areas. Farm families found new goals, and came to believe that these were the reasons they had come in the first place. And now, we are told, to understand the pioneers we need to understand their religion, their family values, their commitment to the health of the social whole. The calculus of risk and gain, and the thrill of chance, seem hardly to be considered. To understand these pioneers we would do better, I think, to look at why people today buy lottery tickets.

And this, Henry, is what I see as I stand here at the side of the road in the deep twilight, looking out over these graves and the land turned and tended by you and your children. In searching for your economic reasons I do not mean to make you less. You were as complicated as I am, and your motivations were as multilayered and inscrutable as my own. Indeed, I am myself made of the same stuff as you, and subject to the same fundamental follies. My life has hardly been more stable than yours. I can't find it in my heart to blame you for leaving this good land. I also have believed in the fairness of a system to which, in the end, I may be sacrificed, and my descendants will not escape the aftermath of my indiscretions any more than I have escaped yours. Will they, with the benefit of long hindsight, wonder why I missed the most obvious facts? The difference between us, of course, is that I can be advised by your life. You cannot be saved by mine, no matter how favorably I represent you in words. To a later age what I write may be as naive as a Butcher photograph, something to be looked through to find the frozen consciousness of another age.

Trees

The unfamiliar furniture of a motel room comes into slow focus. Somewhere in the night, I think, I have dreamed about Henry and Elizabeth.

The café this morning is full of farmers with their seed company caps. In farming counties like this they are meeting now in local restaurants throughout the Midwest, as though they were some giant committee. This is spring, and a lot of the talk is about the weather and planting. Farmers are one of the few social subgroups for whom a conversation about the weather is more than a verbal gesture. I find their talk and accents a comfort. From the time I became an adult my life has been spent in cities, and mostly indoors. Many times, however, I have been gripped with a sudden, wrenching melancholy when I realized that I did not know, at that exact moment, what the weather was like outside, and that it did not matter for anything I had planned for that day what the weather would be. This primitive attachment to the conditions of some small part of the thin envelope of atmosphere around our planet runs deep into the bone. The weather is like an old friend. We seldom meet, but I am infinitely interested in the state of its health. When my family gathers around my hospital bed at the end, and bends to hear from my cracked lips the final words of insight about the human condition, they will probably hear me ask "Will it rain?" If I am lucky they will construe it as a profound concern about the moral climate of Western civilization.

This will be a travel day. The next stop is in Illinois, just over the Iowa line. A single word of oral tradition tells me that I must eventually go to Erie County, New York, but that is a big place, and oral transmission is fickle. I could use more pointers. I hope the intermediate stops provide me with some details.

That will be tomorrow's problem, however. The destination for today is a matter of record. Henry and Elizabeth were married in Illinois, and their first children were born there. Some of those children were still alive when I was young. Although they could not have had enough geographical awareness to have known where in the continental United States they had been living as toddlers, they had learned their birthplaces as a kind of litany, as you or I might know our telephone numbers. They were able to parrot the information to later generations. Some of them knew their place of birth as Warren County, others as McDonough County. They must have been so near the county line that the reckoning could have gone in either direction. A cousin of mine stopped there once and was able, without too much trouble, to find the grave of Henry's father. I estimate that Henry and Elizabeth spent about ten years in Illinois. I haven't the slightest idea why they came to Illinois, or why they left, but the process was not in the least unusual. Many of the early settlers in Nebraska and Iowa came by way of Illinois and Indiana. It was a generational whistle stop for the western migrations.

The day promises to be another warming day. There is, to my thinking, no finer time of the year to be on the plains. Many spring days are quite temperate. The weather is unpredictable, though. There are spring blizzards, and, when the season has advanced, tornados. But for the most part the lengthening days are ones of recovery from the effects of winter. The strength of the warming on days like this is only known where the extremes are wide. I have watched the thermometer plunge more than 50 degrees Fahrenheit in three hours, and it is not unusual to see the temperature rise from below freezing to the low 60s in the course of a day. Such ranges are unimaginable to the person living in a climate tempered by an ocean. After several half-hearted attempts to get out of the ground while the early spring swings through its extremes, the crops seem to erupt from the soil. Trees that stood spring-budded for weeks will explode into leaf in one afternoon. Tradition has it that people in the Midwest who die of old age most often die in the spring. A quick count of my own ancestors who died natural deaths shows that over half departed in the spring of the year. It is easy to imagine that this vernal vigor would be too much for a frame subdued by age and weakened by a long winter. These detonating spring days can rip soul from body as easily as I could snap the head from a dandelion.

The committee on the weather is still in session when I pay and leave. In half an hour I am back on the interstate, heading for the Missouri River crossing at Omaha. The miles begin to roll by. One of the sadder aspects of the interstate system in the prairies is the way that it camouflages the subtleties of the landscape. It is hard to feel the land's gentle changes through so much concrete. The spectacular road system that crosses the Rockies, on the other hand, masks nothing: to insulate the traveler from the heaving topography of the Rockies requires a passenger jet, and even then eyes are mystically drawn to the ruck of rock passing below. Out here, however, the whisper of the land can be muffled by too much pavement. Even the Missouri River slips underneath almost without notice, so smoothly does the road become a bridge and then a highway again. I am 125 years down in the vertical dimension of this pilgrimage, though, and the Missouri crossing has to be at least noted, if not respected. This, and the Mississippi that I will cross this afternoon, were not usually fordable. They were, both of these rivers, physical and political boundaries of some magnitude before this century. Bridges over these rivers did not exist this far south; the pioneer generally sought a ferry crossing. There was enough difficulty in this maneuver that the rivers represented brackets around segments of the migration. While not the baptism of an ocean voyage, traversing a river was still a Jordan crossing, a symbol of a new life in the land of promise.

On the eastward side of the Missouri, after climbing the bluffs, the land changes. If the knolls of eastern Nebraska were waves, these are tsunamis. The hills on a farm become farms on a hill. I know that by the time I get to Des Moines, halfway across Iowa, the land will settle down and become the flat tall-grass prairie which will dominate the next 400 miles. Even here, among these gigantic nubs of soil mountains, the uneven land has been tamed by a mathematical conception of ownership. Bemused by the rigorous geometry of this environment my mind spreads out over the generational landscape of families and genealogical records. There will be no other story about Henry either to learn or tell until I reach Illinois. I can disengage from the horizontal dimensions of travel for the rest of the day, and let my mind travel through another landscape. The safety rope is there if I need it.

As with most hobbies, genealogy is valued both for the product itself and for the state of mind produced by intense work on the product. One of the poorer ways to describe the state of awareness achieved by the family historian, however, is to look at what is produced. A written genealogy is a translation of a complex genealogical mentality into a medium of expression that threatens to simplify it to the point of meaninglessness. The translation suffers from the limitations of the literary medium. A book is, by its very nature, a sequential narrative: it is read from one end to the other. It forces the variform consciousness into a deadly linear format. For those who know the code, the book becomes an encryption of a more complex structure that is encoded on one end and decoded on the other, with, one hopes, minimal loss of content. But it is a difficult translation under the best of circumstances.

Take the most obvious genealogical structure, the tree. A tree is not a linear structure. Suppose that we wanted to turn it into a linear expression. We would go over the tree, touching every branch and leaf, and recording them in a notebook. We will be doing, in the lingo of computer science, a *tree traversal*. It can either be done with a depth-first or a breadth-first technique. In a depth-first traversal ("depth" in this case refers to the up-down dimension and not to direction: it could as well be called a "height-first") we climb the tree, notebook in hand, beginning at the main trunk. We write down the name on the main trunk, presumably the person or couple whose descendants we are describing. When we reach a place of branching (the children of the progenitor), we take the branch on one side, say the leftmost branch. We write down in our book the person this represents. Now we are faced with the problem of whether to continue with this person's siblings or with this person's children. Since we are going for height, the children get the nod, and we take the leftmost branch of the next generation up. This continues, favoring always the next generation over the siblings, until we come to a twig with no branches (no known children). Our notebook now has a continuous list with each person representing a succeeding generation. We have quickly reached the top part of the tree by ignoring most of the branchings. We remedy this deficit by backing down the tree until we come to the most recent place where we chose a left branch, and take the next branch to its right. If we took the leftmost last time, we now take the leftmost except one. (A colored thumbtack would be helpful here to mark which branches we have already taken, so that when we back up we will get the next branch in left-to-right order, neither skipping nor repeating.) We write down in our book the name of the person on this new branch. If the most recent person we had recorded in the notebook had siblings, this new inscription would be one of those siblings. If this sibling has descendants, we must now follow the tree up to the furthest descendants of this sibling. This means that the next person listed will not necessarily be a sibling of the previous two; it could be child of the second sibling. When, finally, we have done all of our climbing up and backing down on a given set of branchings, we will have listed all of the siblings and all of their descendants at that particular branch. Now we back down the tree to the previous generation and repeat the process. When we have covered all of the descendants of the rightmost child branch of the trunk person, we will be finished. It is easy to see that we will cover all persons on the tree using this technique, and that, more significantly, the linear listing in the book will have the persons on the tree encoded in a way that moves across the tree from left to right. If we had stood back and watched someone else climbing the tree in this way, and if we had drawn the tree as the person traversed it, we would have sketched the tree with a general left to right flow. Actually, the pattern is more like what we would get if we fixed a windshield wiper at the base of the tree and wiped left to right.

What we have just done is known to the software specialist as a *preorder traversal*. It is called *pre* order because we did not visit any child before we had visited that child's parent. By changing the plan a little we can get other orders of traversal. We could, for example, visit the children before the parents. That would be a *post* order traversal.

All such recipes are staples of the computer programmer. They are all depth-first traversals because we go for height over width, and they all give us a general left-to-right coverage. But there are also ways of traversing the tree that choose width over height. For a breadth-first traversal we alter the climbing technique. As before, we start with the progenitors on the trunk. When we come to the first branching, however, the method changes: we write down all of the persons whose branches radiate from the trunk. This means that all of the children of the first couple will be listed together, whether or not they have descendants. This will be a complete list of everyone in the second generation. We now choose one of the branches, perhaps starting with the leftmost branch again. Climbing onto that branch, we write down the names of all of the subbranches. Instead of following any of these subbranches, as we did in the depth-first approach, we retreat and follow the branch of the next person in the second generation. We write down the names of her children. The advancing and retreating continues until we have inscribed the names of everyone in the third generation. For the third generation, we do the same, giving us the complete fourth generation list, and so on. It is easy to see that, although we are going to be doing a lot of clambering about, we are nevertheless assured that everybody at the levels below where we are at any given moment are listed in our book. If we stood back, again, and watched this process, drafting a picture of the tree as the leaves and branches were listed, we would find that the tree would be constructed in a clean sweep from bottom to top, as though the tree were behind a windowshade being lifted.

There are other ways to traverse the tree, but these two—the depth-first and the breadth-first—are the ones most commonly used. When we are done with any of these procedures we will have a complete and linear list of the individuals on the tree. Both listing methods are used by genealogists.

The depth-first list was used a lot in the last century, and is still used in a chart known to the hobbyist as a "descendant chart." The breadth-first technique is represented by the standard "record plan" format recommended by modern genealogical societies. In either case, the problem is how to arrange this linear list so that the reader is able to reconstruct the tree. For a descendant chart, indentation is used to suggest the tree structure. For a record plan genealogy, a numbering system and direct ancestor list is used.

There is, of course, much more to the mental discipline of ancestor collecting than the problems of trees and linear encodings. Bird-watching is not about having a five-second view of every species of bird in the world from a distance of less than fifty yards with ten-power binoculars, though a formal approach might make it sound like that. Nor does the writing of genealogies consist of only the mathematical problems of coding and decoding family trees. One major problem with a purely formal approach is that genealogical hobbyists, I am convinced, don't deal in anything like perfect trees. Even if they wanted to, the state of the evidence wouldn't permit it. What they really have inside their heads is more like a network than a tree. Certain nodes on the network are more anchored than others. They can usually make something treelike out it by grabbing an anchored node and shaking it, but the tree shape is more of an afterthought. I have seen genealogists, for example, become so interested in what they call "collateral" lines that the actual line of descent being studied becomes just one of many strands in the finished product.

But the biggest problem with a formal approach is not the shape of the mental space. It is the problem of narrative: what most of us are studying is not a bloodline but a story. I have heard that poets will construct a poem around a single phrase haunting their thoughts. Writers see a photograph and a novel will fill in around it. Ancestor collectors often start with a story. It could be a story they heard as children, or a story endlessly retold at family gatherings. From these beginnings the story builds, the generations build and backfill, and in the end some formal order is imposed on it all. But the narrative, however overlaid, is still there at the beating heart of what they write. If it ceases to beat, the final product will be as dead as the ancestors they have collected.

Good genealogies have been quickened by the desire to follow a church group, or trace involvement in a political movement, or to account for how a building, creek, or lake came to have a certain designation. A peculiar middle name has been followed for half a dozen generations. An old diary, with no literary significance, becomes the focus of research. Someone else in town has the same last name and we wonder what the relationship might be. These are all beginnings. And as the story develops, other ideas well up, flow alongside, and mix with the first waters.

The presence of the story is what makes genealogy hard to write. The rest, the construction of the sequence from the network, can be learned by rote. The real problem is how to follow and develop the narrative. It is so difficult that it is a wonder that it gets done at all. I have known many hobbyists who couldn't seem to pull out of the data-collection phase. The problem is, I think, that the lines of narrative never jell. When it gets too bad, you do what I have done: chuck it aside and go on a pilgrimage, hoping to bring back the initial sense of joy and curiosity, and find the tale whose telling will bind the scattered lives of a family line.

Cousins

After a forgettable franchise lunch on the edge of Des Moines I have begun to tackle the three-hour drive to the Mississippi. Were I following another family—even another of my own families—Iowa would have something to say. But for the Luthers it was just a state to cross, as it is for me today. My goal is the groves of Illinois on the other side of the river. Not only Illinois lies ahead; there is also the Civil War. It sits in the distance like a line of building thunderheads. I can see on the horizon a small dark band lit by flashes of lightning.

The decade that Henry and Elizabeth spent in Illinois was the 1860s. Half the years of this decade were the war years. Even their presence in Illinois probably had some relation to the war. Everything that happened in the United States this side of California during the first half of that decade had something to do with the war. One of Henry's brothers, who came to Illinois with him, joined the Union Army in 1861. He survived a saber cut at Upperville, Virginia, in 1863, and was mustered out in 1865, at the end of the war from a unit that had seen nearly continuous battle duty. He was as loony as a coot, some say as a delayed result of the saber wound, when he died in a mental institution thirty years later. A powerful man, he sat in the asylum tearing his overalls into strips, chanting like a lover plucking leaves from a daisy. It seems right, somehow, that a person who had seen major conflicts of that war at first hand would want to methodically demolish the apparel of civilization. To wear whole cloth after the Great Hacking was a travesty only sanity could hide.

We will analyze the Civil War as long as we exist as a nation. There will be movies, and documentaries, and books, and reenactments until the end of our time. Our appetite for hearing about that war is insatiable, I think, because it is impossible that we could ever redeem the contradictions of it. Even our lives get rounded with a sleep; but the Furies we awoke in that war will chase us past the grave. A minimally necessary condition for a definitive perspective on a war is that there is a winner. Since we could not have a clear winner and still maintain one rejoicing nation, we have tried to make a principle, and not a part of the nation, the winner of that war. The two candidates for this exculpating principle have been the doctrine of federalism and freedom of the slaves.

The slavery approach doesn't work well. Emancipation only became a major rationale after the war began. Lincoln's first approach—Frederick Douglass helped convince him of its absurdity—was to repatriate the blacks to Africa, most of whom had been Americans longer than many of the residents of Lincoln's home state! Then Lincoln wanted to buy all of the slaves at a generous rate and free them. But property that gets bought this way is just higher-priced property. There is, to say the least, some confusion here between manumission and repentance, between the blood of bulls and goats and a clean heart. His last solution, one he sought to avoid, but the one which circumstances ultimately dictated, was a war of liberation. But are there just two silly solutions and one good one to the problem of human slavery? If the only way to establish the rights of a race not to be property was an armed conflict, why did blacks achieve this in almost every other nation by the turn of this century without a major civil war? If the dignity of a race was the winner of the war, why did substantial progress on the social and economic equality of the races go into a ninety-year eclipse after the war? Though slavery is intertwined with many of the deep causes of the war, the evidence suggests that simple opposition to slavery cannot stand as the full rationale for the war, then or now.

The other hypothetical winner of the war was the national concept. Before the war the states were small nations, and the nation as a whole was a confederation of conflicting and sovereign entities. After the war there was a strong federal system. So it is said. The problem with this is that the war only accelerated a process that was already well under way. There never has been an absolute answer to this problem of regional and ethnic differences versus the national unions that encompass them. Political life will be forever a matter of compromise and conciliation, of tradeoffs between one set of goals and another. It is the use of war as a tool in these conflicts that is the problem. Is there any evil as great as a civil war? Even as I travel today, one of the largest and strongest nations on earth has dissolved, and we hope daily that horrors of civil war can be avoided. Can we hope this and still claim that the American Civil War was justified by the spin it put on the federal/state posturing of midcentury America?

If we should lay principle upon principle, as though we would wall ourselves off from the brutal events of the Civil War, we will never encompass it with our whole understanding. As I move eastward and down through time the turbulence increases. Tomorrow I will begin to move under it, to the quieter days of an adolescent republic, but for the rest of today and tomorrow the land will have no quiet.

One aspect of that war which has captured our imaginations is the image of the divided family. Hundreds of thousands of families had reasons for sympathizing with both sides. Who knows how many families contributed sons to fight on both sides? Tens of thousands of first cousins must have passed through the sights of each other's rifles. We reserve a special repugnance for a war that breaks the bonds of kinship. All war, however, breaks some of these bonds. How strongly and closely we are related to each other by ties of blood is one of the surprises awaiting the amateur ancestor collector. The odds that any two genealogists, put in a room with all of their notebooks and charts, will find a connection in their ancestral lines, are surprisingly high. I marveled at this when I first began work in family history. I once took the trouble to work out some of the mathematics of it.

The problem, as I posed it, was to ask how likely it was that any two North

Americans taken at random share an ancestor within the scope of a given number of generations. To understand what is being asked, we need to think about another tree. What we were talking about earlier was a tree of descendants. Another tree form shows all of the ancestors of a given person. The ancestral tree spreads out as we go *back* in time. Since we each have two parents, it is a binary tree, and spreads in a relentless and regular way into the open sky. We are supposed to have two parents, four grandparents, eight great-grandparents, and so on. There is a limit to this tree, however. If, as is commonly believed, humans are all descended from a small initial group, perhaps a single pair, then any tree continued far enough will eventually stop spreading and begin to contract, since at the top of the tree everyone has the universal parent set. Clearly, then, while we may have 8 great-grandparents, and even know their names, do we really have 1,024 great-great-great-great-great-great-great-great grandparents? For most of us the answer is probably no. The reason we don't is that cousins marry. When single* first cousins wed, they rob their descendants of part of their full ancestry, since they share with each other one of their grandparents. Between them they have seven grandparents instead of eight. That seems like a small loss, until we project it backward. The lost grandparent means a loss of only two great-grandparents, but by the time their family trees are extended back nine more generations they will have lost over a thousand ancestors from their combined progenitors. If this matters at all to you (if it doesn't, consider on what ground you might object to brothers marrying sisters), realize that the social situation will eventually excuse kinship intermarriage for all of your remoter ancestors. They would not have been able to find a partner who could prevent the pruning of the ancestral tree. The available mates would all have been kissing cousins.

I distinctly remember wondering, sitting there in my Sunday School in Nebraska, where Cain got his wife. I have a suspicion that he may have saved his brother from incest when he invented murder. The early generations

---

*"Single" in this context means that they share a single grandparent. Double first cousins share two, etc.

from a small founding group have little choice. They can marry their siblings or cousins or parents or uncles, or they can commit genetic suicide by bearing no children. It takes several generations before they have the luxury of choosing a mate who is not *known* to be related. Even then, genealogy would not be a popular hobby. After a couple of generations back, everyone would have the same family tree.

As the tree of successive generations spreads outward and downward from a starting pair—it must be thought of as growing downward if we let the ancestral tree control the orientation of the metaphor—the marriage options open up. Besides growing downward, the tree of descendants is unlike the tree of ancestry in another important way: it is not a binary tree. Couples can average more or less than two children per parent. It has the potential of quickly getting wide, though the Four Horsemen have often served the purpose of containing sections of the tree which spread too far and too fast. Only in the last two or three centuries, in fact, has the growth rate approached anything like the binary tree of ancestry with its doubling in each generation. So we have two trees, the tree of descent and the tree of ancestry, working together to make up a complete family tree. If you want to get a picture of what the genuine article is like, try holding up your index and second finger in the traditional V for victory sign, then place behind it your other hand, making the same gesture upside down (I lock the steering wheel with my knees to try this). Your top hand represents the tree of descent. The bottom hand is the spreading triangle of your ancestry. The diamond shape you see between the four fingers is the real shape of your family tree. As you move your hands up and down, you can see that the diamond gets wider when it gets longer, and vice versa. We are all far enough from the ultimate ancestor that we have the illusion that the further back we go, the more ancestors we have, but this is clearly wrong. A correctly drawn family tree slows its spreading at some point. The factor of how early the outside edges of the tree of ancestry slows its spreading as we work backward is closely related to the cousinhood of individuals. It is the place in the middle where the grand squish begins that tends to make cousins out of persons who don't know each other. And the crunch comes much sooner than is commonly imagined.

68

What is the likelihood that the driver who just went around me, glaring at me for wandering out of my lane, is a definable cousin? If we shared a grandparent she would be my first cousin. If we shared a great-grandparent she would be a second cousin, and so on. What range of cousinhood would be the best guess? This is not easy to compute for the real world because of changing birth rates, immigration, and shifting pockets of group intermarriage. It is a calculus problem with an immense number of free variables. By ignoring most of these variants, however, it can be reduced to a simple combinatorial problem. If I have no first- or second-cousin marriages in the bottom part of my family tree, chances are that about 300 years or thirteen generations ago, the gene pool that I represent was spread out over 2,000 persons all around the world. The other driver would also have 2,000 such ancestors. What are the odds, of the hundreds of millions of people alive then, that one person was in both sets? Here intuition fails us. Working it out as a combinatory problem, and accumulating the odds through the generations (it took me a whole morning when I tried to calculate this: I am not a mathematician), it looks to me like the odds are over fifty percent that she and I are at least ninth cousins. I'm sure she would not have glared so if she had known.

It is clear, though, that general figures tend to lie in these matters. The chance I would be so closely related to someone from an inbred population, such as one of the Ainu of Japan, for example, would be much smaller. In the same respect I probably have a larger chance of being related to any of the North American mongrelized populations. Running the same numbers through U.S. population figures I find that the odds go over fifty percent fully fifty years, or two generations, earlier. So I am probably her seventh cousin. There is another number that makes the rounds: we are commonly said to be about six or seven degrees of consanguinity from other people. I do not know the source of this statement, or even what range it applies to (other North Americans? others of the same race? all persons?), or whether it is a limit or average. My own numbers suggest that seven to nine would be closer as an average. Either way, however, we are an exceedingly inbred bunch of feuding cousins.

Another way of coming at this problem of kinship suggests that the consanguinity numbers may be closer to the lower figures. This way is less precise, more anecdotal, but it allows me to avoid some of the constraints that elude a simple mathematical modeling. I wrote a computer program which simulated what would happen if a fertile, twenty-year-old couple arrived on a large island and found themselves to be the only inhabitants. I wanted to see what the blood relationships would be after several generations, assuming no other persons came to the island, and none of the islanders left. I set up what demographers call *life tables* to control the probability that in any given year a person might marry, might have a child, or might die. In the beginning the people were allowed to wed and bed anybody from the opposite sex who was of an age to have children. After the population was large enough I restricted potential marriage partners by introducing an immutable incest law. I wasn't sure what relationships to include in this law, so I consulted the page in the Anglican *Book of Common Prayer* entitled "A Table of Kindred and Affinities Wherein Whosoever are Related are Forbidden to Marry Together." I found some of the restrictions curious, and, more significantly, hard to program. In the end, I just forced everyone to marry outside the immediate family (i.e., outside of their siblings, their parents, and their parents' siblings, their grandparents, and their grandparents' siblings). If I had the slightest idea why the *Book of Common Prayer* decrees that a woman may not marry the brother of her deceased husband, I suppose I could have included it, but it seemed more realistic to put this restriction down as a cultural aberration and leave it out of the simulation.

When I started the program off, and the years began to tick away, I was surprised how slowly the population grew. Because I was using random numbers correlated with typical probabilities to decide when things would happen, I had no way of knowing ahead of time how this microworld would develop. In the first few generations the question of whether the simulation would work at all was in the balance. All too often the population simply died out. Sometimes the first couple failed to have enough children, sometimes they had too many useless males, sometimes they had no children who survived to adulthood. Often the first couple succeeded in getting a second generation going, but then the new generation would fail to continue the line. There were too many such instances, and I had too little patience: to make it work reliably I found I had to cook the books in the first few generations by raising the fecundity and lowering the death rates. Even so, it was not unusual for the poor islanders to struggle on for 200 years with the whole project in doubt. There were many stretches of several years where there were no fertile couples, just people past bearing and children too young too bear.

The wonder that there is anybody on earth at all, writing or reading this, is a matter to ponder. It would have been so easy in the first centuries to bring the human project to nought. I wonder how many Edens there were before one took? There was perhaps an Eden where Adam and Eve failed to figure out how to have children. And another where Eve had all boys. Perhaps a third where the children got huffy about incest a little too early. Another where the first couple decided to postpone parenthood in favor of self-realization. And so on. Why do we think that it all had to work right the first time? There is little enough evidence that the Lord God does things that way today. Experimentation, if that's the word, is the rule rather than the exception. Miracles are permitted, but they are not standard issue. I am tired of hearing how likely it is, because there must be so many inhabitable worlds, and the odds favor the development of life on more than just this one, that there must be other intelligent life in the universe. Who knows what the odds really are? They may be vanishingly small. Perhaps we should be amazed that, out of the billions upon billions of chances, it happened at all. The cosmos may be littered with false starts. The apparently limitless universe of worlds may have only made something that verged on sheer impossibility—the development of human life—slightly more possible. If we understood the odds, we would perhaps be in a better position to appreciate this improbable sequence of events. Perhaps we would be less inclined to put the outcome in the balance again. The universe may not be big enough to let it happen twice.

With a little orchestration, then, the population of my simulated island would usually reach the takeoff point after a dozen generations. Within a few more generations there would be hundreds of people. Soon there were a couple of thousand. Once the island was fairly well populated, I had the program simulate and tabulate a large number of courting events between strangers to see how closely related, on the average, potential mates might be. Suppose that you were one of the people on this island, a male, twenty generations removed from the first couple, and that you were walking along the beach one day, enjoying the solitude and mulling over the question of why you were there at all. Coming toward you is a female you do not know. You are sure that she is not your sister, your mother, or your first cousin. Suppose that, due to the strong incest laws, the first topic of conversation on such occasions, after the requisite exchange about the weather, is a comparison of family trees (it's my paradise, so why not a genealogist's paradise?). What is the most likely relationship of that person to you? It turns out that chances are greatly in favor of her being a close relative, only one or two generations out of the range of intimate relations, a second or third cousin. She might be further removed, in the most extreme case by as much as nineteen generations, but this would be a rare encounter. Even if, early in the history of the island, the inhabitants had split the population into exclusive subgroups with strong miscegenation laws, it would only have lowered slightly the odds that she was a near cousin. Such is the result of an isolated population.

The earth is just this island, its population a bit bigger and further removed from the first parents, and the cousins therefore a little further apart, but the same secluded place. We may indeed be one and all within six or seven degrees of blood relationship to the entire human tribe. This dubious legacy of the Civil War, that families should arm themselves and fight, annulling even the bonds of love and blood, is one that sits as a blot on our national record. I do not know how to excuse it, other than to note that all wars in this century have been between peoples only slightly more removed from the bonds of kinship. It would hardly be prophetic to predict that the next few wars will be fought between the same cousins. To halt this internecine slaughter we desperately need some images of family that are stronger than the ideologies which lead to armed conflict.

Warren County, Illinois

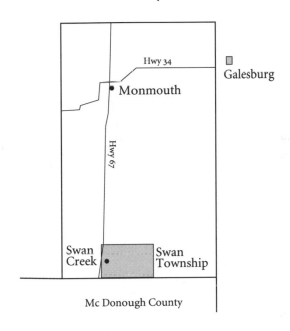

Remembrance

Thunderstorms loom as I near the Mississippi crossing. The cloud line is moving with me, though, so I will never feel the brunt of these storms. They will track ahead of me for the rest of today, and be gone to Indiana in the night. No prairie child can look on these spring storm fronts indifferently, though. There are unwanted visitors from the skies this time of year. Although more people are killed by lightning than by tornados, even here in the Midwest, we can be as blasé about electrical death as we are terrified that the whirling wind will carry us off. I have wondered why there is such a flourishing business in the patent medicine of lightning rods, when the real fear, ready for some entrepreneur to capitalize on, is the funnel cloud.

The span across the Mississippi, like that across the Missouri, is disguised as an uninterrupted interstate, but it is a more notable crossing. You can't pass over the father of waters accidently. Its volume here is nothing like the mass of water flowing under the bridges one or two states further south. The Mississippi is a tamed river, with dam over dam as you go upstream. But when it gets to St. Louis the taming is more illusion than reality. If this river gets mad, it will go where it wants. As I cross these creeks and rivers my attention is always drawn upstream. There are people, I have heard, who cannot cross a river without following it in their hearts to the calling ocean. My experience is the opposite one. I usually want to follow it to its source.

In a curious way I am moving this afternoon into a more advanced society, even though I am moving back in time. The life of the Nebraska frontier was much like life at any American frontier through most of the nineteenth century. For a hundred years you could have chosen a life that was substantially the same as your parents, if only you would move to the edge of the westward advance. I am following a family that presents itself as the paradigm of a restless and progressive people, always on the move, choosing the risks of the edge rather than the stability of the center. In actual fact this family, by hewing to the edge of advance, managed to keep their life style unchanged for nearly seventy years. In terms of social and technical development, this family was more conservative than progressive.

In the 1860s, at the time Henry and Elizabeth were in Illinois, they were about ten years away from the frontier. This part of western Illinois came under the plow as early as the 1840s and 1850s. The urn-shaped state, as Donald Culross Peattie notes, "began to fill up from the bottom, like a vase." At the bottom is a tangled knot of major rivers, the interstates of the early settlers. By the time the Luthers arrived society here was just moving out of the early frontier stage. It is possible, for example, that Henry came to Illinois on a train. There was probably more passenger service, to more towns, than there is now. If he brought his family in a wagon, he may have come along one of the planked toll roads. Prices paid for land would have reflected the inflated values caused by two and three turnovers. Existing houses could be bought or rented. The real frontier in 1860 was behind me more than a hundred miles. The Luthers were headed to the edge, and would, with the dubious results we have already seen, find it, and abandon their descendants there, but while they were in Illinois they were in a phase of practice for the frontier rather than on it.

The place I am looking for is south of the interstate about sixty miles. There was a scenic road I could have taken from Iowa that wound up and down the Mississippi bluffs, but today I am taking the faster Illinois road. If I get to the county seat around supper time, I may find the town library still open. In many of these Midwestern towns the genealogical societies put their materials in the local libraries. In the East the societies are more likely to have their own buildings, reflecting a more advanced conception of the art of genealogical research. They have to process larger numbers of us. West of here the genealogical resources can be minuscule outside of the court houses. When I was in Saline County yesterday, for example, I found a single three-foot shelf in the library. The librarian told me that there was no substantial, nonprivate collection of materials in the whole county. Here in the Midwest the conditions for genealogical research in the smaller, less populous counties is unpredictable, but it is often tied into the library in some way.

Monmouth, Illinois, is the county seat of Warren County. As I expected, the courthouse is easy to find. It is a strange Victorian structure with a touch of Richardson Romanesque. The towns here lack that sense of long decline present in so many towns further west. Here the growth was less malignant, and the decay, if it came, less dramatic. There is, however, evidence that there has been some negative change in the economic base.

The library is open for part of the evening, as I had hoped. Even more fortunate for me, the genealogical society has a special room that is available whenever the library is open. The urge to know is upon me like the Philistines upon Samson. Supper and the motel can wait. I shake myself from a hypoglycemic stupor and lug my notebooks down to the basement room.

A member of the local genealogical society is just finishing her work. She is helpful and knows exactly how to answer my questions. Obviously she has been at this for enough years to be able to adjust her answers to the background of the questioner. There is a meeting of the local society here later, but for the next two hours the place is mine. I have done this enough times that I know where I should start, but I can't resist a few minutes of shelf walking. It will tell me what is here, and stamp the geography of the room into my brain. Occasionally these local societies will have collected a valuable research tool which you would only expect to find in a major library. Nothing here, though, is out of the ordinary. The real value of the collection is its concentration on the local population.

As a first step I pull from the racks the earliest county plat map to find out

77

what were the political divisions of the county near to the time that interests me. Counties in the last century were like states in current mental geography. They were the place you were from, or were going to, but when you were in them you belonged to a town, or, more often, a township (the population was overwhelmingly rural). Knowing the township layout is essential for the interpretation of many types of records. There are multitudes of townships in the United States, of course, and the names show almost no originality; they only had to be unique within the county. I am looking in particular for a place the family histories call "Swan Creek," where Henry and Elizabeth were said to have been married by "Squire Simmons." In the southern part of the county I find it: next to the border of McDonough County is a Swan Township with a village called Swan Creek.

The second step is to go over a row of local genealogies. I am looking for the biggest deposits of ore first. Finding something on Henry and Elizabeth done by another genealogist would be a major strike. The families I have researched have usually been less than notable, however, and have, with few exceptions, been the sort who came and left. I seldom find myself in an opened mine. This evening is no different. Nothing here at all, to judge by the titles of the genealogies, so I start scanning their indexes for the surnames associated with Henry and Elizabeth in this county. Genealogists are especially dismayed by collections of family data with no indexes. These family memoirs often contain photographs, newspaper clippings, will inventories, transcriptions of old letters, and, above all, the oral traditions and stories that are the family's verbal treasures. They fall somewhere between a family scrapbook and a serious genealogy. That they lack an index is a sign that the writer had little participation in the more formal aspects of the hobby, and little consciousness of the community of other genealogical researchers. More often than not the target audience is a group of grandchildren and great nephews and nieces. Such works would not even have been preserved in libraries were not for the foresight of local librarians with a sensitivity to county history, or an active genealogical society with a penchant for collecting unrefined data.

My next step is to look at the county history. Bulky county histories exist for most U.S. counties. I have never seen a complete description of the process that brought these mammoth tomes into being, but they are so universal, and so similar, that it is impossible to take them for what they present themselves as: a history of a county. Relatively few publishers are involved, and they seem to have published little else besides these county histories, many of which were issued for the 1876 U.S. centennial. Sometimes editors and compilers are not even mentioned on the frontispiece. I suspect that at the end of the last century the publishing industry saw a chance for a handsome profit in vanity publishing. These county histories have, as essential addenda, long biographical sections listing the major figures in the county. Apparently writers were sent on rounds to every family identified by some local newspaper as worthy of mention. They collected whatever information the family was willing to give. Usually the information had an ancestral component. It was this biographical section that guaranteed the profit of the venture, for every one of these families could afford, and would probably buy, a copy of the county history to show to their friends and relatives. Sometimes these families even paid a fee to have their listing included.

Since the book was masquerading as a legitimate history, the first half had to be filled up with historical materials. Such volumes begin with an extended description of the region's geological development and land features. For most of these descriptions, a standard geological narrative was only slightly altered to fit the local geography. You could write a mythology of nineteenth-century geological ideas from the material in these sections. They have all of the standard components of orogeny, glaciation, erosion, and hydrology, thoroughly blended and baked into a pseudoscientific cake that could not possibly have been digested by the majority of the readers, even when the ideas were current. It is totally unpalatable to modern tastes. Next comes a description of the Indian past, based on nineteenth-century anthropological legends, full of exploits that are long on color and short on archaeological reality. Another common component of the early chapters is a canned U.S. history, followed by a history of the state, probably purchased at minimal cost from some underpaid academics. The history of the county itself, when we finally get to it, is usually in the final sections of the work, and seldom occupies even half of the nonbiographical text. It often consists of all of the anecdotes about the county's early days current in the parlors, barber shops, classrooms, and business establishments of the main towns. The extent to which they were good stories, and not the degree of their authenticity, caused these tales to make the rounds. The publishers of the county histories did us a favor by writing down stories that might otherwise have been lost. They are an invaluable comment on the attitudes flourishing in the early town life of these counties. Where they do offer the odd fact, they may have preserved sources unavailable today. Handled correctly, these histories can be of value to both historians and genealogists, but as serious histories most are impostors. Some, whether through accident or effort, have a modicum of scholarship, but such cases are more notable for their relative rarity.

Few of these hasty histories contained an index, an unnecessary expense for a profit-oriented publication. So librarians, local historians, and genealogists have undertaken to index the histories in most counties. One of these indexes is here in the Warren library. I discover, to no surprise, that the Luthers receive no mention in the county history biographies. They passed through here years before the history was written, and left behind no descendants, so there was no profit in mentioning the small roles they might have played. There is a listing, however, for a son of Hezekiah Simmons. From the description I can tell that this Hezekiah was the Swan Creek "Squire" from the family history. Everyone written up in these miniature biographies sounds like God's gift to public life. Simmons appears, nonetheless, to have cut an unusually fine figure in the early public and social life of the county. I note with interest that he brought his family here in 1838 from Buffalo, New York. That's in Erie County, and the association of Swan Creek with Erie County through a name kept in our family is not to be overlooked, so I dutifully record the entry in my notebook for future reference. Anyone who has traced pioneer families becomes aware that names socially associated with target names, whether in a neighborhood, a church, or through a marriage, are often important pieces of evidence. They are sometimes the only evidence about where to look in the search for a family's previous habitat. We are dealing with people who may not have had the foresight to leave their name on any public document that would survive a hundred years. They trusted instead soft sandstone grave markers and family memories, both of which inexorably erode with the friction of time.

It is an interesting question to pose even today. If the press of mortality was upon you, where would you leave your name, and some data about your fleeting life, so that someone two hundred years from now could uncover enough about you to enliven a genealogy? This is assuming that you are one whose name will not be of interest to the standard historian. You have to rise high to be able to rely on historians. There were, even in this small county, many who thought that they had imprinted their names and lives on a community in a way that would achieve social immortality. They may have survived for these first hundred years in county histories and the various editions of *Who's Who*, but they are just part of the general statistics to even the most detailed of essays in major historical journals. Think about how these ordinary people would endure a major transformation in the historical base. Suppose no one who lives in this land a hundred years from now spoke English, or that there was a shift in political life that made old political and social boundaries obsolete. Many a Celtic druid imagined that he would forever figure in the history of the British Isles. Hezekiah Simmons, let's face it, would not make it around too sharp of a bend in the political road. Think how hard it is to get remembered, then, if you could not even claim the status of a local notable. "There were many widows in Israel in the days of Elijah," Jesus noted, "and yet Elijah was sent to none of them, but only to Zarephath, in the land of Sidon" (Luke 4:25–26). Where will you leave your name so that you will not just be one of the unnamed? Gravestones are unreliable things, especially in a world filling up with people and a limited amount of arable land. The *bigger* you build a monument, the more likely it is to be noticed by those who would plunder it for the stone itself. The more you write on it, the more likely it is to end up as a clever inlay in some future garden wall. Hardly a pharaoh in Egypt rested easy for longer than a century in his mammoth pyramidal tomb. The more modest you make a headstone, on the other hand, the more likely it is to escape notice and be lost. In land like this, where there is reliable rain for cemetery grass, the soil level can rise several inches in a century. I have seen standing stones no more than a century old half-buried in the soil. In some older cemeteries there may be a flat plaque now buried from sight for every upright stone. I know a genealogist who brings her husband to graveyards to witch for buried stones. He often succeeds, perhaps not so much because of his psychic powers as because of the number of buried stones.

I'm sure people who, like me, have been part of this search for the insignificant have seen their own lives, at one time or another, in the same light, and have fantasized what they might do to help out some future researcher. If you care about the trouble you might cause some prospective investigator of your life, here are some ideas. First, get your name in the paper as often as possible. So many fields of research have gone back to these old newspapers that they have become one of the most well-preserved types of documents from the last centuries. Newspaper itself falls apart in a few years, but almost all of it ends up copied and recopied on microfilm. Some of it, the *New York Times*, for example, even gets indexed. You don't have to make the big-time rags, however. If your dog gets a cold and has to be taken to the vet, call the local news desk. Second, get arrested. An unbelievable avalanche of documentation is set in motion with this simple act. It would take a court order, in fact, to get your name effaced from the records. From a documentary perspective, you are wasting your time going to all of those Rotary meetings and being a good citizen. Third, buy land. There is not now, nor will there be in the foreseeable future, any general statute of limitations on the time that land records have to be preserved. I have a dream that I will someday go to all of the counties where my known ancestors lived and buy a small parcel of ground as near as possible to the ancestral lands. Since you can style yourself as you choose on these deeds, I would list my name as "descendant of . . ." After holding the land for a few months, I would sell it. The record of purchase and sale is what I want, not the land itself. In the deed I would leave enough of a trail to get a researcher to my current address. In this dream I also sell these dozens of properties for a profit. I am, after all, the great-grandson of a notorious real estate gambler.

Now that I have covered the secondary sources, the county history and local genealogies, the next job is to pull together the picture from the primary sources. A few of the records, such as church registers and business directories, are right here in the library, but most are in the courthouse and will have to wait for tomorrow. Indexes to many of those records are here, however. The local society has been hard at work. I find row lists for most of the gravesites in the county, and a nicely indexed set of church records. They have also put together a transcribed copy of the 1860 census. I know already that Henry and Elizabeth are in the census, but having clean copy enables me to find some records of Henry's siblings that had escaped my notice before. By the time I leave I have begun to put the picture together. A later trip may allow time for more detailed consideration of what is here. It couldn't all be done in one pass, even if I had the whole day here. At a later time there will be some names I know that I don't know now, and those names will lead to new ideas, which in turn will lead to more names, and so on, the image emerging from the background through many passes over the same records, as though this were a brass rubbing instead of a set of documents. This first rubbing tells me that I am not going to have an easy time of it tomorrow. The image has been nearly effaced. My people were just folks passing through at a chaotic time.

A Warren
Record

The sounds of military drills disturb my dreams in this land of war. It was during the Civil War that Illinois emerged as a national power. These fertile, newly plowed lands at the western terminus of the railroads were for the North what the Shenandoah Valley was for the Confederacy. The difference was that there was no General Sheridan here trying to smash the agricultural base of a warring people. Illinois land is heartland. It has never been host to a battle in any major war.

The courthouse opens early, and I start to work as soon as the clerks have arrived to unlock the offices. I'm not trying to get a detailed picture of Henry and Elizabeth from these documents: the source material for such an image probably has not been preserved in these records. What I am hoping is that something here will aid my search farther east.

Henry came to Illinois as a young man in his father's house. Almost immediately Henry married Elizabeth Cline, who as a girl had traveled to Illinois with the Luthers. The way the family is listed in the 1860 census makes it clear that the family center shifted to Henry and Elizabeth as soon as they were married. Henry is listed as the family head on the census, and his aged parents were sheltering within the new family unit. This fits well with the perception of Henry among his descendants: that he was a take-charge fellow who was always willing, and often able, to bear the concerns of his kindred. He was the glue, I believe, that held together the caravan of Luther siblings, who came out from the East and, after stops in Illinois and Kansas, ended up in Nebraska. Henry and Elizabeth were the stuff of dynasty.

What I know of Henry's father Ebenezer hints at a personality different from that of his son. Born in 1797, Ebenezer married Aurilla Wait in New York in the 1820s. They had at least seven children. Two stayed in the East, five came west. Ebenezer died here in Illinois at the age of seventy. Aurilla lived to be nearly eighty, and spent her last years in Nebraska. After her death Henry and his siblings took the separate paths which were to fragment the memory of the eastern homelands among Henry's children. Not more than one or two of Henry and Elizabeth's children could have known their grandfather Ebenezer in Illinois. His stories, if he had them to tell, are lost; the trail of his personality grows cold here. Not even a single story *about* Ebenezer has come down in the family. All I know about him through the family, beyond the obvious genealogical data, is that he was a Free Will Baptist. Ebenezer was not, whether by dint of a weak personality or by trick of circumstance, the beginning of a line of descent. He was the end of an older line. In this transitional land my attention begins to alter its focus from Henry to Henry's father. Ebenezer is the one I want to glimpse in these Warren County records.

I try the Recorder's Office first, where vital statistics, listings of birth, marriage, and death, are kept. Only the marriage records reach far enough into the past to be of any use. This is a problem I have encountered before. In the move from the church to the state as the preserver of remembered events there was a period where birth events failed to find any place of record. When the church was the recorder, the birth or baptism of children was the occasion for marking their presence in the official records. Many of the new churches in the land of democracy, especially ones that abandoned formal birth rituals, eventually ceased to keep records of birth. Some who did try to keep such records lost them as the waves of immigration carried away the congregations. Local governments did not step into the breach right away. In many of Midwest counties birth records only start up after 1870. Official death records were begun even later. Only marriages, which were perceived in a civil as well as a religious light, were reliably recorded.

From the marriage licenses filed here I see that most of Ebenezer's children married in Illinois. Matrimony was as much a preparation for the frontier as learning to hitch a wagon, break sod, or dig a well. Pioneering was a business whose minimal incorporation size was the partnership of the marriage bond. In the early surge of exploration the family had been effectively excluded. The hunters, trappers, and drovers who pursued their business in this place had to dodge or escape the marriage bed. Whatever families there were came through the "country wives," the Indian concubines. For the waves of settlement, however, the rules reversed. Successful pioneer farming was a wagon that required a team of at least two strong pulling animals, and every extra shoulder was welcome. So these marriages in Ebenezer's family, in addition to the overlay of love and courtship, were also a yoking up for the work ahead.

Henry and his siblings show up in a few records, but for Ebenezer I draw a blank. There are no probate or court records. Land and tax records, one of the last refuges in a search for the insignificant, also yield nothing. It appears that Ebenezer did not even own the land he lived on. Since it is possible that he was missed in the indexes, I try a direct search of some of the major records. Still no luck. I always watch for other Luthers, however. If I'm looking for Ebenezer I'm also looking for his siblings and relatives. There *are* some other Luthers in these records, but for most of them the townships where they lived or the dates in which they owned land do not suggest any connection to the family I am following. It is a frustrating morning. But in the afternoon the hours of digging pay off. The index to the land records lists a transaction for John Luther in the year before Ebenezer arrives in Illinois. On chance I track it down. There on the deed is Ebenezer's name! He is listed as "the only brother and heir of John Luther, deceased." Ebenezer is selling a piece of land that John had purchased with a bounty certificate received for his service in the War of 1812. John acquired the land through patent in 1818. Ebenezer, still living in the East, sells it through an attorney in 1859.

I have been in genealogical libraries when investigators, after years of search, uncover a long-sought piece of information. Their behavior can be shameless. Archimedes, sitting in the spa and watching the water displaced by his body flow over the edge of the bath wall, could not have felt the same rapture as some of these researchers experience. I was elated, but there was no one around to share my pleasure.

Before the afternoon is over I have refined two nuggets of geographical information from the land record. First, I found out where in Pennsylvania the family had stopped after leaving New York. I knew from the family history that Ebenezer and Aurilla had spent at least a dozen years somewhere in Pennsylvania. Now, thanks to the John Luther deed, I knew it was Crawford County, about halfway between Pittsburgh and Lake Erie. Ebenezer was living there when he sold John's bounty land. From some earlier scanning of census indexes I had suspected that Crawford County might be the area. Now I knew. Meadville, Pennsylvania, the county seat of Crawford County, would be my next stop. The second piece of geographical information I found when I correlated the land record with information in the book *War of 1812 Bounty Lands in Illinois*. John Luther, it says there, had instructed that his correspondence be sent to Clarence, New York. Clarence, the map tells me, is in Erie County, about fifteen miles east of Buffalo.

And this was all I found during a whole day in the Warren Court House. If the deed had not been there, I would have finished the day with almost no new information to help me on my way. On the other hand, there could have been more. There is no way of knowing the probabilities involved. It comes, or it does not come. For my part, it is a step on my way out of the wilderness. The cloud of smoke goes before me by day and the pillar of fire by night.

City of
Water

Soon after sunrise I am on the road back to the interstate. The sweep of the storm front on the night before last left behind a cold high-pressure area. The air is beyond clear. It almost seems to have a telescopic force on the horizon. The big sky effect, so marked in Nebraska and the western states, is missing here, so the magnification of the horizon causes a further closing.

It will be a full day to Pennsylvania. The facing sun will be well at my back before I'm in Crawford County. For Pennsylvania, where genealogy has attained a high degree of development, I have a guidebook that tells me that the Crawford genealogical library is closed tonight, so there is no rush. A day away from the records will help me to refocus what I am doing out here. It is such a temptation, in the blush of discovery, to turn this into another collecting trip. The collecting part is too familiar. Pilgrimage is harder.

If I am a pilgrim, I should be stopping at shrines along the way. Since Lincoln is the local deity, I should be veering south to Springfield, but I can't afford the time. I trust Abe won't take it personally. Funny how gods get addressed in such familiar terms. A distant cousin of mine on my mother's side grew up in the area I am traversing today. He tells how he and his chum, strolling home after a grade school pageant for Lincoln's birthday, were conversing about how Mr. Lincoln had walked several miles to return an overcharge when he was postmaster at New Salem. An older lady passing by heard him use the term "Mr. Lincoln." She stopped the boys and, with all the sternness she could muster, reprimanded them: "Please! You wouldn't say 'Mr. Jesus,' would you?"

The morning's travel will be dominated by Chicago. All of Illinois along Interstate 80, from the middle of the state on, is directly affected by Chicago, for better or worse, as is most of the northwestern quarter of Indiana. I lived in Chicago for many years. We had a saying then that you were from one of two places in Illinois: Chicago or the rest of the state. Those who carry on the social habits of the rural Midwest avoid the place, and those who live in Chicago hardly ever travel downstate. Today I will give the city wide berth, but its shadow will lie over my way until the afternoon.

Chicago was my first big city. When I was young my head was full of wonderful abstractions about cities. They were invigorating, alienating, cultured, urbane, decadent, liberating, necessary, and impossible, depending on the latest sociological mode. Having lived in and out of them for half a lifetime they have become much less abstract. They just are, without adjectives. Cities have fair claim to be a part of the furniture of life, as much as the country. They will not damn us, and the rural life will not save us. The opposition set up between Chicago and downstate, or between any city and its rural matrix, is partly fiction. One depends on the other. Think what you will about Peoria, Galesburg, or Mattoon, they exist in unique symbiosis with Chicago. The method and practice of farming is conditioned by the presence of the Chicago market. If Chicago were not there, the rural culture of the Illinois farmers would be changed also. We might as well post pictures of Bauhaus blocks around our fields to remind corn why it grows.

If you were to draw a map of the North American Midwest which represented its topographical features, then plot on the map the major cities and centers of population, you would quickly observe one of the controlling perceptions of the nineteenth century. The social patterns of city building today, which seem so bound up with road and rail, were regulated by another mental mechanism when the cities were founded in the last century. Surface water plays a small role today; then, however, it was the center around which civilization revolved.

The Midwest of the 1800s was served by two massive drainage systems. One of them pulled the water south: dozens of large and navigable rivers tie into the Mississippi watershed and mix their waters with the Gulf of Mexico and, eventually, the southern Atlantic. The other was a lake system. The Great Lakes are the largest inland body of water in the world, and water in them flows into the northern Atlantic. As settlers issued from the eastern regions after the American Revolution they followed these two aqueous tracks. Even today the continent's large cities are mostly on one or the other of the two systems. The boom that was Chicago was occasioned in large measure by the interconnection, at that point, of the two drainage systems.

Did any city in the world ever grow like Chicago? It was the most predictable and programmed boom of the last century. Next to Chicago even Phoenix looks like a town planning accident. As the Frenchman Michael Chevalier noted in the 1830s, Chicago, then home to hardly more than a couple of thousand people, had been planned and plotted almost thirty miles out. Land within that range had been divided, parceled, sold, and resold with a view to the eventual expansion of the city at the intersection of the water systems. Lots in Chicago were numerous enough to hold more inhabitants than were contained in any large city in the world in the 1830s. Chevalier noted that a buyer of these lots would "probably esteem himself fortunate if on examination he shall find not more than six feet of water on his purchase." Chicago's mother was water and its father was speculation.

Of all that has been written and said about the changes between life in the pioneer period and life today, the biggest difference, I have come to believe, is in the attitude toward water. The provision of power from an outlet is not so life-altering as the flow of water from a tap. The century and a half of material development since the pioneer period has served to reconstruct the mental space of American life, and the single greatest change in that universe of concept has been in the way we relate to water. For the pioneer, water was the great shaper. Homes were built to account for the flow of water. Water had to be available for drinking, cooking, washing, and cleaning. Livestock consumed astounding quantities of water, and perished quickly in the Midwestern heat without it. No family of settlers could be far from water. But to be near water is to risk its malevolent side. Flooding has engendered more destruction than all of the earthquakes, winds, and storms put together. Only fire can compete with it. Water in the form of ice and snow brought a yearly reckoning to farm life, and winnowed the merely tentative settlers from the resolute pioneers. From the days when the last mile-high glaciers retreated into the Canadian hinterland, up to the beginning of this century, fresh water was the absolute and decisive constructor of the Midwest landscape.

The earliest settlers worked *with* water, not against it. Francis Grund, also writing in the 1830s, referred to the people in the Midwest as "amphibious," and the settlers as "half horse and half alligator." They had a sense of water that rivaled their sense of weather. They knew where it was in their sleep, and dowsed it in their waking step. Many of these abundant lands I am crossing now were wetlands and swamps when the Indians were here. The topsoil was a sponge several feet thick. Only the upper few inches ever dried. Grass and sedge thrived here because they loved the drowning water (The rice that grows in flooded fields across southeast Asia is a relative of grasses). Land transportation became impossible in the spring. At the first thaw most of the Midwest turned into a sea of mud.

The seasons and whims of water were not convenient, however, for a land filling with people and dreaming of progress. The construction of a road—a good, straight, usable road—is a refutation of the water-formed land through which it passes. It is a statement that, come flood or mud, I will go there, and be there on time. When the road reaches a swamp, the road must be raised or the swamp drained. Where the road crosses a river, it needs a bridge. If the road is not to twist like a whipworm river, the features of a land fashioned by water must be suppressed. Water is fluid, and the lives accommodated to it have the ripples, gyrations, and undulations of a liquid existence. The civilization being constructed in this Midwestern water garden was not prepared to conform its dreams to the fickle ways of water, and so, stream by stream, dam by dam, levee by levee the great water system was tamed, so that roads would run straight and feet would remain dry. The master became a slave.

If you were to think of this as a public works project, it was surely the largest single project in the last century. If you include in it the construction of the highway system in this century, it may be the largest public works project in human history. The trillions of dollars we continue to spend on water control alone are hidden in military budgets and in budgets for roads, farm subsidies, dam control, and natural resources. If the pioneers had seen it as a single engagement in a campaign they would have shrunk from the fray and pulled back into the East. Fresh water, however, is like the primeval forest. It can be conquered, for the most part, acre by acre. A few large wetlands and rivers held out from this piecemeal enslavement and required the marshaling of a larger army, but for the most part the engineering prowess of the farm family sufficed. It is significant that a large portion of the modern task of controlling the water system was left to the Army Corps of Engineers. It was warfare, and its major battles were conducted over a whole century.

The plans of the early pioneers took into account their place in the hydro-logical cycles. Little of our modern mode of existence gives it a second thought. Such transformation of the mental landscape sets us at large re-move from the life of the early settlers. If we would travel along the paths of their vanished world we must see the divinity of water through their eyes. Those who would write the history of this part of North America in the nineteenth century should all be sent to the water wilderness of northern Canada to survive for a few weeks, to make the acquaintance of water where it is not in total submission to the technology of civilization. Life has a different feel there, and I fancy that this feeling is not unlike the sentiments of our ancestors who first pushed into these lands.

And so, as I coast eastward, and under the tumult of the Civil War, the lines of another struggle emerge. The ground becomes damp, and the moisture-laden air of Indiana and Ohio rises into the afternoon sky. The road itself becomes a concrete river, and the steering wheel the helm of a river barge. I am seized with nostalgia for a life which respects the force of fresh water. The flow wants to carry me away from my storm line. I steer against the pull of the water.

The Probability of
Actuality

Chicago is now behind me. I passed the industrial complex around Lake Michigan an hour ago, and am halfway across Indiana, moving through a mixture of fields and groves. I may be backtracking along the same route that Ebenezer followed when he came to Illinois.

He may have come by train. Some of the east-west railroad lines were constructed in this very strip where the toll road runs, across the late-settled land between the two drainage systems. The first waves of pioneer settlers to these lands, however, made use of the National Road, which lies about a hundred miles south, bisecting the states of Indiana and Ohio. Some German ancestors I have researched would have been on the National Road in the 1820s and 1830s. When I get to Crawford County I will be in genealogical country that I know well, though tracing Luthers through that region will be a novelty; work on my German ancestry has made western Pennsylvania a familiar territory.

If you are a North American, chances are, unless most branches of your family tree veer off into other countries at an early stage, you have an ancestor who was Pennsylvania Dutch.* My own tree is heavily populated by

---

*"Dutch" does not refer to The Netherlands. It is an Anglicization of the word the Germans used for themselves.

these people: Rodabaughs, Klingensmiths, Studebakers, Pitsenbargers, and the like. They were all products of the great German migration into the middle Colonies. The majority of immigrants between 1730 and 1850 were probably Germans. The ones who came before the Revolutionary War pioneered the cultural milieu that we think of as Pennsylvania Dutch. They became such a potent political force in Pennsylvania (composing perhaps a third of the population) that Benjamin Franklin was concerned—probably unnecessarily—that they would upset the old political allegiances of the Quaker/English regimes. When the lands over the Alleghenies opened up after the War of Independence, the Pennsylvania Dutch surged into the fertile lands of Ohio, Illinois, and Indiana in great numbers. The grandchildren of the Germans that excited Benjamin Franklin became a worry during Lincoln's Illinois campaigns of the 1850s. Though their mere numbers threatened political destabilization almost everywhere they lived, the Pennsylvania Dutch and their descendants were for the most part quiet farmers with neither the motivation nor the political savvy to assert a cohesive national presence. Albert Bernhardt Faust points out that in the earliest foothold of Pennsylvania Dutch culture, in Germantown, near Philadelphia, it was necessary to resort to fines and the importation of English civil servants to supply the area with holders of public office. Few of the Germans would voluntarily hold positions of civic authority. Political noninvolvement would continue as a characteristic of the Pennsylvania Dutch culture until the Germans became integrated into mainstream North American culture. Not until the middle of the twentieth century was a person of solid Pennsylvania Dutch descent elected as a U.S. president.*

The story of the Pennsylvania Dutch does not belong to this pilgrimage, but there are still German elements in it. Henry's wife Elizabeth was a second-generation German surnamed Cline (or Klein), whose parents were

---

*I am referring to Dwight Eisenhower, whose parents were from the pacifist River Brethren group of the German Baptist Brethren Church. Herbert Hoover on his father's side was ultimately descended from a Pennsylvania Dutch family (Huber), but his Quaker parents, both of whom died before Hoover was ten, were culturally far removed from the German tradition.

both born in Germany, but the Clines were probably not Pennsylvania Dutch. Relatives who knew Elizabeth as an old woman say that she could still sing German lullabies she had learned as a child. The family history also tells me that Ebenezer was of "Dutch [i.e., German] and English parentage" but annoyingly fails to remember whether the German element came through his father or his mother. You might think that Ebenezer's father would have been Pennsylvania Dutch, with a name like Luther, but this is improbable. Few Pennsylvania Dutch had Luther as a family name. The large majority of people in North America with this surname derive from a 1635 Puritan immigrant from the south coast of England.

Most of my own experience with genealogical research has been with backward tracing through lines of descent, a motion from the present into the past. This is not true of all genealogical work. Quite commonly lines are traced forward from a progenitor through his or her descendants. In North American research this would mean at least some of the work would take you from east to west. I have often pondered the question of whether it is harder, on the whole, to follow lines of descent up or down, east or west, through this land. To work backward in time means that evidence must be found in the place of research that would lead you to an earlier residence. To work forward means that some hint must be found of where a family has gone.

If the approach is a brute force search through some exhaustive listing of people—a census, for example—then, all other things being equal, it would be easier to work backward, since in previous years there were fewer people spread out over a smaller space. But things are rarely equal. Earlier censuses tend to preserve less information than later censuses. On the other hand the censuses before 1860 have all been indexed, and the indexes have been put into computerized databases. But it is seldom necessary to look at the issue this abstractly. Time-consuming physical searches are the last resort. What we would rather find is some specific evidence that takes us directly from A to B, or at least narrows down the field of search to the county and township level.

In east to west tracing, going forward in time, we hope to find citations about where a family went. We might find, for example, that someone in the west had fallen heir to some eastern property of an older relative. The will itself, or the court records from the probate process, might have mentioned where the western relative was living at the time of the bequest. If immigrants did not get all of their eastern land sold before they left, a proxy sale could have created a record with a crucial current address. As a last resort, we can count on the fact that people usually went west to places where cousins already lived, or, if the territory was entirely new, they might have traveled with a group of people from the same location.

To trace west to east, backward in time, we can look at wills again, since the immigrant might have included a legacy for an eastern relative. Many references to newly arrived settlers would have included the place they came from ("the Hite family from Lancaster County, Pennsylvania"). Censuses from 1850 on gave the state in which the person was born, and both birth and marriage records began to include the parents' places of birth. Family oral tradition commonly preserved some memory of the eastern homelands. And the fact that families came in clusters from one place to another can also be useful to the researcher following a family from west to east.

All in all, I think that tracing backward may be easier for most immigrating families. It is easier because the data is more likely to be there, at least on this continent and in the nineteenth century. I don't know if this holds for all types of genealogy, but I suspect that, with appropriate exceptions allowed, it might be some kind of general rule in genealogical tracing. It happens because people have more of a sense of where they have come from than where they are going. One takes priority over the other. I was walking across a college campus last summer. As I passed two individuals who had just stepped up to each other, I heard a snippet of their conversation. The first one said, "Where are you going?" The second said, "Man, where are you coming from?" And as I walked past that piece of dialogue, and the rest of what they had to say to each other faded into the background noise of the street, I noted the protocols of conversation at work. It is not generally considered to be polite to answer a question with a question, but the rules of conversation, like the rules of parliamentary debate, allow for certain questions to take precedence over others, so that if a question with higher precedence arises the first is shelved until the second can be dealt with. The question of where a person has been, if it is an issue, generally takes precedence over the less conversationally pressing question of where one is going.

This disparity between the significance of the past and the future is not a difference in kind. It is more a difference in degree. The way in which we know the past and the future is remarkably similar. Some have tried to stress the difference, claiming that one, the past, is real, and the other, the future, is not. But the difference between the past and the future is not on the level of reality. They are both real. We will *have* a future, just as we will have weather tomorrow.

It is the *content* of the weather and the shape of the future which interests us, of course, and not its reality. If the light at the end of the tunnel turns out to be the fires of Hell and not the radiance of angels, it will make a difference. Since a description of the future can't be in terms of certainties, we express our perspective on the future in the language of probability. Talk of the future is couched by its very nature in the discourse of probability.

When we talk about the past we are in the same situation, only we are less aware of it. Our discourse takes on a mood of certainty, and we fail to see that we are using the language of probability. Alfred North Whitehead used to argue that the way we referred to both the past and the future was a subspecies of statistical language. The difference in mood between the past and the future was more an issue of *actuality*, in his way of speaking, than it was of reality. The future is real, it just isn't actual. Both the way we imagine something will come to pass, and the way we construct it as an event that has already gone by, make use of the same types of reasoning.

This is not the place to try to explain, even if I could, how to get into a philosophical posture that puts us in a place to compare discourse about the past and the future without invoking a strained notion of reality. Whitehead's *Process and Reality* is not that hard to read: consider it footnoted here. The main difference between the past and the future in our perception may simply be that it is easier to figure out where something has been than where it is going. A lifetime of experience reinforces the idea that we will find the pieces of evidence that lead to the past more readily than we can find and interpret evidence about the future. It is just a slight shift, but it is enough. A drop of a few inches per mile is enough to keep a river moving. The probability that we will be right about something in the past is just a little better than the probability we will be right about something that we think might happen to us in the future. Both projections are notoriously unreliable. Probability causes reliability to fall off as an exponential function of its distance away from us in time.

This can be illustrated rather nicely by a well-known genealogical problem. Suppose that you have an agnate line that goes back ten generations. These are all fathers. In most North American cultures they would have your surname all the way back. Unlike mothers, fathers have an intrinsic uncertainty about them. Your mother claims that he was your father, and the conventions of society would lead you to believe that he was your father, but any evidence that was too explicit would begin to conflict with our list of permissible customs with respect to sexual behavior. Let us say, without prejudice against your mother, who I am sure is a faithful wife and true witness, that on the average one out of every one hundred such claims to paternity is false, a conservative estimate. The odds that your father is not your father are then one percent. But what are the odds that your grandfather, the father of your father, is not your genetic grandfather? These are the odds that your father is really your father times the odds that your grandfather is your father's father, or ninety-eight percent. That is not too bad, and no reason to skip a Christmas card to the old man. Take this back ten generations and you gain a new respect for the power of adultery. The odds that a chart of your paternal line is correct about your ninth grandfather drop to less than ninety percent. That is, there is a one out of ten chance that the name in that position on your chart is *not* your blood ancestor, assuming an average infidelity rate of only one percent. An infidelity rate of five percent, which looks more realistic when you consider pre-Victorian sexual behavior, leaves you with only a *fifty* percent chance that the actual blood relationships agree with the chart that far back. If you had a chart that went back twenty generations, through both male and female lines, and which had a reasonable spread (not a lot of intermarriage), only about half of the people on that chart would have a chance of being in the blood relationship defined on the tree if the infidelity rate were a mere five percent.

This falloff factor means that uncertainty grows quickly as what we know recedes from us. Both time and mediating events create a fog into which the events of the past and future disappear. But the fog behind us is less dense. Although the probabilities are poor and are multiplied rapidly against each other, the past has, it seems, an ever-so-slightly better chance of fitting our image of it than the future. This increase in the odds cause the past to seem overwhelmingly actual in comparison with the future. A river is, neverthe-less, a river, even though it has an upstream and a downstream. Just so, there is one reality underlying both past and future, and our perception of the past and the future is a part of the same mode of knowing.

This has been a major change in the way the world presents itself to me. When I was young, the past was absolutely given and the future seemed absolutely free. But it is no longer so, and I don't know which is more unsettling: to understand that we are forced to use our imaginations to construct the past, or to think that the future is not totally open, that it is full of events whose high probabilities make them almost inescapable. For me, in this year and in this state of mind, the second is perhaps more disturbing. I have grown accustomed to a history that is a collection of more and less probable stories. The balancing and evaluation of evidence that is a part of the free play of the reconstructed past comes more easily than it once did, and the lack of certainty is less troubling. But the unreconstructable aspects of the future sit heavily on my mind. The part of me that once wanted to change the world begins to wonder if it can even change itself. The actuarial tables tell me that I have a two percent chance of dying this year. Step by measured step the unimaginable becomes the unavoidable.

Colleges

A written notice marks the Indiana-Ohio boundary. The lay of the land does not change. This reminds me of a trip to the West with my parents when I was a child. The dreary landscape of the desert terrain provided no evidence of the political boundary between Wyoming and Idaho. Sagebrush stretched from one horizon to the other. A sign at the actual crossing read "This is not Wyoming sagebrush. This is Idaho clover."

It will take about four hours to cross Ohio this afternoon. Ohio and western Pennsylvania were the first Old West for the American Colonies. As settlers began to push over and past the Allegheny barrier after the Revolutionary War they found these wonderful, fertile Ohio lands. Ohio till land may be the best farm land on the North American continent. Year after year, with no irrigation, the black soils bring forth an abundant crop.

Thoreau, traveling in a coach on his way to begin a canoe trip in the Maine woods, pointed out that "he who rides and keeps the beaten track studies the fences chiefly." To anyone from the New West (Illinois and west) one of the first oddities to be noticed when driving across the secondary roads in the fertile Ohio lands is the *lack* of fences. Through most of this journey everything has been fenced, mostly in barbed wire. Fences reflect a use of the land which alternates either in time or space between crops and animals. In the Far West, where animals dominate, and here, where crops are sovereign, borders are less significant. There is little rotation of use, and so little need for fencing.

This is the domain of the great American forest. It was said that a squirrel starting in eastern Pennsylvania could go west from tree to tree and not touch ground until the Mississippi River. I have been in this forest all day, but there is something about Illinois and Indiana that makes the stands of forest less daunting. Here the idea of forest is assertive in a way that it was not back there. Stop cultivating a field here and in a few years you have a mature forest of beech, oak, walnut, and maple.

My first few trips across this state were on this northern road that I travel today. It moves through the less comely parts of Ohio: the industrial sections huddled under Lake Erie. I know that this is as much Ohio as the farming communities, but I find it especially jarring today to be confronted with the detritus of an early twentieth-century manufacturing region. Except for the communities concerned with lake transportation, this northern tier of Ohio was the last to be settled. Like Illinois, the state filled from the south.

Only in the last decade have I traveled south of this road and experienced the good Ohio lands which were the magnet that drew the Americans over the mountains. How the Germans from Pennsylvania loved that land! Even ones who had not seen the German homelands for three generations recognized that it was the land their customs and culture had been designed around. The collection of forces which later pulled them on westward, away from those lands, must have had a power past all description. Not everyone who found a home in these lands moved on, of course. Two million people came here before the Civil War, and the majority probably stayed. Of those who made this land their family home, many were Pennsylvania Dutch.

The Germans had a love of education that paralleled their affection for farm life. They founded colleges *everywhere* in these lands. There is a college or university in about every town of respectable size. What Massachusetts was for the north, and Virginia was for the south, Ohio became for the entire trans-Appalachian United States after the Civil War: the hub and heart of higher education. From 1860 until the middle of this century this region was the breeding ground not only for presidents and politicians but also for university presidents and department heads. Those inhabiting the lower echelons of academic life in the West must have imagined that Ohio was one great campus.

Looking up from here to the present puts into perspective how quickly the educational establishment has grown. In the United States and Canada there are currently 3,000 to 4,000 institutions that grant some official postsecondary degree. A *million* professional educators inhabit their halls. At the time I travel through now, the 1850s, only a few thousand educators served a population of 20 million, barely 1 college teacher for every 10,000 individuals. Today about 1 college teacher exists for every 300 people, a thirtyfold increase in occupational density. Another way to look at this is to imagine that you were at a party, and the guests had the same distribution of occupations that you find in the United States at large. What are the odds that, if there were 20 guests, one of them would teach in a college or university? The answer is fifty percent. The probability that you would be able to pick a male college professor out of that crowd is some obscure function of the size of the weave in his tweed coat.

When we take into account educators at all levels, from kindergarten to graduate school, the number of North Americans for whom teaching is their main employment is several million. If we include support personnel from administration, maintenance, student services, and so on, it would not surprise me if 10 million people were part of the business of education, and take their main employment from it. The yearly budgets of these institutions must be well over a trillion dollars.

The size of the educational enterprise in the United States and Canada still understates its social role, however. The university is one of the three seminal, autonomous components of North American society. For any person living north of the Rio Grande there are three parallel institutions around which society is constructed. One is the civil life embodied in the political and economic systems. The second is the church. And the third is the educational establishment. These are not only handy intellectual divisions of the complexities of human social life: they represent self-perpetuating social organisms whose wholes exceed their parts, and whose goals transcend the individual purposes of the constituent members. We may have inherited these institutions from the Europeans, but they came into an interrelatedness in this hemisphere which would have been impossible in the old country. In Europe these institutions were huge solitudes, each trying to deny and suppress the other two, and succeeding at certain times and in certain places. On this continent they entered into a unique symbiosis. They were posited as separate but related institutions, each one an undivided part of the whole of social meaning, but each in a state of active confrontation with the other. As Garry Wills points out, everything in the U.S. Constitution was anticipated in European cultural history: "We invented nothing," he claims, "except disestablishment." The older cultures of Europe wanted to know, perhaps, whether a society composed of these ingredients was forever doomed to the waves of total warfare which have racked their world since the Reformation. We on this continent have always been the Great Experiment. From the days when the Puritans put up their first crude huts around the cradling shore of Massachusetts Bay we have been a people in a glass house, John Winthrop's city on a hill. The world has watched to see what would happen to a society founded on self-contradiction.*

To begin to understand the social role of the university in North America we must place the symbiosis of these three institutions into historical perspective. It is perhaps more correct to speak of the Great Experiments, in the plural, since the mutual relationships of church, university, and state have had at least three distinct configurations in the last three centuries. One version of the mix is, of course, the nation we currently are. Now that my pilgrimage has taken me below the time of the Civil War, however, I can see a different nation. In Canada the change from one form of nation to another was more politically obvious: the regions of Canada began to come into the modern confederation after (and perhaps because of) the Civil War. In the United States the nuts and bolts of the political system did not change, but

---

*Although I intend this description to include both the United States and Canada, the relationships of church, state, and university are somewhat different in Canada, where the distinctions are less ideologically explicit and the institutions are less confrontational.

the spirit energizing the mechanisms of government altered profoundly in the 1850s and 1860s. In my drive this afternoon I have come, not to the younger days of the modern nation, but to the waning days of an older conception of nationhood, one that began in the middle of the eighteenth century and continued until the Civil War. Before this phase of nationhood is a still older national consciousness, represented in the United States by the various colonial regions and in Canada by the early French-Canadian culture. In each of these three periods the basic social institutions have remained the same, but their changing interplay has given the period its distinctive consciousness. It will help later on if I give names to these three temporal subnations. Let's call the first one the Foundational nation, the second the Transitional, and the third the Modern. The Modern is behind me now. I have just entered the Transitional period, and the Foundational lies ahead, over the horizon, past the end of this pilgrimage.

Each of these three phases of North American society has seen the dominance of one of the three institutions. In the Foundational nation, religion was the most significant player, with civil life ascendant and the university playing a subdued role. In the Transitional period the government and civil life gained an enlarged role, and the educational system was beginning its rise to prominence. In the Modern period, the university has become a potent player, at the expense of the public influence both of religion and of civil government.

The nature of the modern version of the experiment produces profound paradoxes in American life. We live in a condition of constant contradiction. Each of the three institutions maintains that it is absolutely sovereign and self-sufficient, while at the same time each is completely dependent on the health and continuance of the other two. We are all, both inside and out, partners to this triple confederation. Most of the North Americans I have known are made of the same raw material. Their lives are in tension between these three poles. They don't know how to make these three sovereign entities fit into a seamless whole, and neither do I. The individuals I have known who have fled one or more poles of this triple peril have only achieved a one-generation calm. Work in genealogy makes you acutely aware of the forms of redress contained within extended family units. Ignore the church and a son will wear the cloth. Turn from education as a useless investment and a daughter will do a Ph.D. in Old English. Refuse to participate in civil life and the religious and educational values of your grandchildren will be taxed out of existence. Better, I think, to face the tension within the scope of our single lives, and *be* the triply contradictory people that the experiment intends.

But to face our conflicts is not to understand them. It is, after all, an experiment. If it had no possibility of failure it would be something else. What meaning there is will have to emerge at the end. "The owl of Minerva," said Hegel, "spreads its wings only with the falling of the dusk." It is the next phase of this nation that will be able to cast some comprehensive interpretation around it all. We will have more success at interpreting the experiment that ended with the Civil War.

It is, perhaps, the shift from the Modern to the Transitional perspective which is behind my ambivalent feelings about Henry and Arthur. If I see them as an early version of the modern spirit, and I like what we are, then they are the honored pioneers of what we have become. If, however, I see them as denizens of the Transitional era who were early examples of the spirit of the Modern period, they are no longer true to their type. Along the way I have acquired an affection for the people and culture of the Transitional experiment from which Henry fled. It is perhaps this that brings me in search of Ebenezer, this that makes me want to break through the dynastic shield. It is a hard thing to straddle a change in the spirit of an age.

Crawford County, Pennsylvania

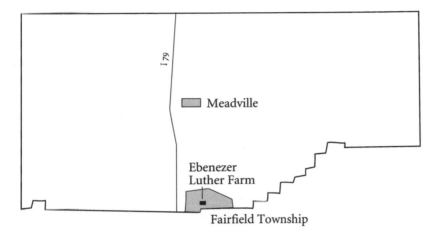

Backwater

I underestimated the time it would take to cross Ohio. The lights of Meadville, Pennsylvania, hide the fainter stars as I exit the interstate. Since this is Friday, Meadville, another county seat, will be my weekend camp. I can use the genealogical library tomorrow when the courthouse is closed, but nothing will be open on Sunday, so my first crack at the official records will have to wait until Monday. My ancestral safety line grows more taut as I approach the next stake. The name on it is Ebenezer.

He lived somewhere around here from the early 1840s to about 1859. I had always imagined Pennsylvania to be a minor transition for his family, but it may have been more significant. The years which he and his family passed in this county may have been the longest period they spent in any one place. Only two of his eight children would have been past the imprinting age of ten when he and Aurilla brought them here. To the other children this would have been home. Crawford County was probably for Ebenezer's family what Saline County was for his son Henry's family.

Ebenezer is a quiet ghost, and a visit with him will be the most difficult one of this trip. He stands on the fringes of my tribe's consciousness, the shadowy parent of a dynastic source. Not even my grandfather, who was already at the margins of my own acquaintance, and who was born in 1870, could have known him, since Ebenezer, his own grandfather, died in 1867 at the age of seventy. The problem is confounded by Ebenezer belonging to what is actually another nation, though it had the same name as the present one and occupied almost the same borders. It is a nation that has passed from the earth. His was the Transitional nation of Daniel Boone, Henry David Thoreau, Washington Irving, and Nathaniel Hawthorne, of Henry Clay and Andrew Jackson.

This is different landscape than the one I traversed this morning. Then I was still in the Midwest. Now I'm on the western fringes of what could be properly termed the East. Land forms in this part of the continent are dominated by coastal plains and the Allegheny ranges of uplands. The coastal plains will have no part in this pilgrimage, but the upland regions will be important. For the past two hours I have been climbing into the west-facing edges of the Alleghenies. The starlight tonight shows little of the land's face, but it is not unknown terrain: I passed by here several times a year through most of the 1970s.

In those years I hadn't the slightest idea that my immediate ancestors had called this home. I remember thinking on those trips that there must have been something wrong with the farmland in the northwest section of Penn-sylvania. The area was so underdeveloped. It appeared that the land had not been able to keep settlers. At that time I wondered if the soil was so infertile or so swampy that agricultural settlement didn't stick. Now I know the problem was more a political and social one than anything to do with the land itself. Where the land around here is dutifully farmed, it yields its harvest.

These were in large part bounty lands. This stretch was called "Donation Lands." They were used to pay soldiers who fought in the Revolutionary War. Certified veterans could apply for papers, called bounty certificates, which allowed them to claim a farm-sized piece of land in one of the sections of the unsettled areas reserved for bounty claims. The certificates, however, were usually valid no matter who turned them in to the land offices, so they were tendered about like bank notes. This was at a time when accepting script was always a little risky. Attitudes toward paper money were quite different in the first years of the American republic. Putting your money in a bank was more of an adventure than it is today. Bounty certificates came to have an important role as currency. Only a small percentage were used in the fashion intended.

The intention was that the veteran should get himself a family, if he didn't already have one, then proceed to the bounty land area, find a suitable homestead site, and use his certificate as valid payment. He would thus have his farm, and would in time become part of the economic life of the new region. In this way the lands newly acquired from the Indians could be filled with a self-sufficient and thriving population. This was the intention; what often happened, however, was that the veteran presented himself to a land company and traded his bounty certificate for, if possible, hard currency. The land company collected certificates and traded them for large tracts of bounty lands. After a suitable markup the company would sell pieces of the bounty lands to settlers who did not have certificates. But the land companies retained sizable portions for speculation, thinking to capture the higher land values of a progressing society. Those who bought lands in these areas, or acquired them by the intended use of the certificates, often found themselves isolated, with large stretches of undeveloped lands separating the farm clearings. This was not a propitious situation. The settlers were not just farmers—they were speculators themselves, with plans to thrive and be wealthy. To develop the land and to sell it at a higher price meant that there had to be a large supply of people who wanted to buy, and a corresponding shortage of lands for sale. But there were always lands to buy in the hands of the land companies, and persons arriving to buy often had their own bounty certificates. Both business and settlement proceeded at a snail's pace. It is no surprise that many of the land companies went bankrupt, and that many of the settlers abandoned their land.

The scenario in this region of Pennsylvania is much more intricate than what I have described. For whatever other reasons might be invoked, however, the results were the same: a pattern of substandard development, whose aftereffects still linger today. People simply did not come in the planned numbers. When coal, which is found throughout this region, became a valuable commodity in the middle of the 1800s, the land's fate was sealed. Already harmed by the intervention of large investors, the conjectured mineral value of these lands, with the corresponding cycles of boom and bust, lifted them out of the framework of stable agricultural settlement.

When looking at a U.S. map one day I noticed that these backwater regions really were backwaters. If you draw a half circle around the outer edges of the Mississippi drainage basin, you will mark many regions of lesser development. From left to right, they begin in Nebraska and Kansas, proceed up through South Dakota, upper Minnesota and Wisconsin, then pick up in the northern tier of Indiana and Ohio, on through to the deep Appalachian regions of northwestern Pennsylvania, West Virginia, and Kentucky. What they have in common is that, as backwaters, they have almost no navigable rivers. They are upstream from the sections that were able to be used for travel and transportation. There was a window of time, after the lands were opened for settlement, and before road and rail diminished the significance of rivers, when the use of the vast Mississippi water system gave a small, crucial bump to the development of midwestern regions. Missing the window doomed many of these areas to a perpetual cycle of underdevelopment, broken only by short stretches when the mining of minerals in these upland regions provided respite from the economic doldrums. These backwater regions are another instance of an earlier amphibious stage of social evolution which has disappeared from cultural expression but lingers on the map.

This week I have transected the half circle of the upper Mississippi and have arrived at the kind of community I know well. The houses are built differently, the horizon looks unfamiliar, and the weather brings enough rain to be the envy of anyone from the high plains of the West, but the community is the same in many respects. It is sleepy, safe, comfortable, friendly, and nearly starved to death. Lack of investment shows up like bones through the skin of an emaciated body. It is better to be poor here than in some of the richer cities of the heartland, though. They haven't much, but the economic restrictions don't carry the stigma they do in healthier parts. These communities at the backwater edges of the Mississippi basin wear their penury with a plebeian dignity.

When Ebenezer and Aurilla were here it was already a social backwater. How ironic that they should have set their family on a path that would lead from one edge of the Mississippi drainage to the other, and in doing so should not have improved the prospects of the family. They were poor farmers on both ends of the upper Mississippi fan. By road and rail they meandered for fifteen years across lands so fine that farmers from minimally fertile areas of the world would have given a cry, leaped from the wagon, and buried their arms in the soil, protesting that they would never leave this Eden for any lesser lands. Ebenezer's family must have felt the pull of the land at every step. If they did not, they were not constructed from the same genetic material that I am. What force, or what collection of forces, was in possession of them that they could not be stayed by the call of fertile land?

In the 1820s a retired British naval officer, Basil Hall, wrote about a visit to the Pennsylvania-New York borderlands just north of here that "there is nothing in any part of America similar to what we call local attachments. There is a strong love of country, it is true; but this is quite a different affair, as it seems to be entirely unconnected with any permanent fondness for one spot more than another." He was watching, at the western frontier, the birth of the new nation which would come to inhabit the boundaries of the Transitional nation, and noted with curiosity the convertibility of land and wealth which made the Modern era possible. It is this great restlessness that I cannot quite get my mind around, the irresistible urge for progress that inhabited these people like a madness. Although some diminishing of this attitude was inevitable as the land filled up at the beginning of this century, it was displaced into a curious colonialism and a rabid capitalism that still haunts our political halls.

A philosophy of increase, which seemed so right for the new country, has lost some of its gloss. Unconstrained growth can be as deadly as no growth at all. My thoughts have more than once been turned to the cottonwood trees of my childhood. Cottonwoods may be the most uncouth trees in the world. In the spring they drop a mess of male flowers that hides the early green of the grass. The bud has a sticky sap that can't be washed from your hands. Once a year the trees send aloft a storm of cottony seeds which build up on the ground like a layer of snow. The aged wood is so dense that it will turn an axe. A two-by-four made of it requires the strength of an adult to lift. In eastern Kansas, where they used cottonwood to build cabins, they called it the "warpingest" wood in the world: a cabin sided in summer with wood sawn while it was green would let the snow whistle in through a hundred holes in the winter. After a cottonwood has matured it seems to draw lightning, and almost every cottonwood over fifty years old takes on an ugly, misshapen form from lightning splits and branches broken by the weight of the dense wood. Unlike other trees, it doesn't seem to have a stable cycle in its mature years. As long as it lives it grows wildly. It kills itself, in fact, by its constant growth. There are few cottonwood trees a hundred years old. But for all of its many faults, it has one overriding virtue: it doesn't need much rain. When it is mature, it sinks its roots so deep that it can draw hidden groundwater. Its leaves also have a waxy texture which allows them to control respiration in the dry heat. Say what you will about its less attractive habits, in semiarid lands with ample subsoil moisture this sensitivity to water is the clincher that gives cottonwoods an ecological niche. The wild growth that dooms a cottonwood may have been an adaptation to allow it to find water sources far below its roots.

When I was a boy my father took me to Algernon—perhaps it was on one of those Memorial Day trips to his mother's grave—and showed me the farm land on which he had lived as a young man. It was the same homestead on which his mother and her family died of typhoid. He had inherited it when still a baby. The soddy was long gone, but on the site were two giant cottonwood trees that my father, and his father, had planted in the early years of this century. They were in their woody senescence, huge and deformed. I see those trees now in my memory as a kind of cipher for Arthur and Henry, and through them as a symbol for the last century of North American society. I don't know whether the cottonwood could have a graceful maturity and still keep the qualities it needs to flourish in its marginal climate. We, in a similar way, nourished in a microclimate of westward expansion, have compensated for the decline of water with a spectacular growth. Our century of expansion is gone, however, and the personality we have developed in this period must adjust to a changed environment. We will eventually, I fear, die the death of the cottonwood if we cannot find a way to bring the water back, to cherish it and not to chase it. William Morris said of his own nineteenth-century England: "I am no patriot as the word is generally used, and yet I am not ashamed to say that as for the face of the land we live in, I love it with something of the passion of a lover." Such a love of place, once ours also, now eludes us.

Tools

The many stops for fast food on this trip are beginning to tell. A weekend out of the car should bring some calm to my major organs. I have been noticing on this trip the specialized equipment for food delivery at the franchise outlets. We have become too familiar with the food preparation process in these places: it is worth more attention. When we walk into a restored blacksmith shop we are confronted with an array of tools whose purpose is obscure. The tool by itself does not tell enough of the story. But if we saw the blacksmith use it, we would know what hours of analyzing the tool itself could not reveal. We see the employees in these food shops working with a large number of mechanized and unmechanized tools. The tools are not observed in isolation from their use. If we inspected them behind glass, but had never seen them in use, we would find most of them to be utterly baffling. My attention was especially drawn to the special scoops used to put french fries in the little bags. They are simple hand tools elegantly adapted for their dubious purpose.

One of the more ambitious attempts in my lifetime in looking at this tool-and-use problem was occasioned by the Voyager spacecraft. It is the first piece of our civilization to be purposely sent beyond our solar system, and so is the first chance we have had to edit ourselves for some alien perceiver. Experts spent years putting together universal symbol systems and artifacts which might convey to another sentient species, without seeing us in person, something about our culture and how to find us. It will be a long trip, of course, so the materials are more of a time capsule than a direct message. It is our far descendants that will be here if they come.

I'm inclined to doubt that there is anyone out there to interpret these items, but if there is, are we sure our children will want a visit? The visitors might be nasty. The trick is to provide clues that would only lead the *right* ones to us. My suggestion would be to forget all of the other stuff, and send along a french fry scoop. Anyone who could figure out what it was used for would surely be intelligent enough to find us. And if they still came after figuring out its purpose, they could only be motivated by pure benevolence toward the children of our sad species.

Morning finds me at the Meadville library waiting for it to open. As I've noted earlier, genealogical societies in the East often have separate quarters from the town libraries. In Crawford County the genealogical collection is in the same building with the main library in town, but arranged in a way that it can keep its own hours. When it is open, there is someone with genealogical savvy at a desk. Access to a person who knows the local records is a real bonus. Librarians sometimes know enough to help, but in many counties all I have been able to get from a librarian was the phone number of a person in town who was responsible for the genealogical archiving. The genealogical librarian in Crawford County is good at his job, and in a few minutes I have my bearings and my notes are spread out on a table, ready for work.

Again I face the index issue. The data in this collection which mentions Ebenezer or his family are just a collection of pointers to a dozen years of a family's life. These ancestors I am chasing were simple people of the land, sunk beneath the level of social self-consciousness we associate with literature and legend. If the worth of their lives were to be measured by the number of pointers to it in archived materials, their lives were beneath price, measured in pennies hardly worth picking up. What is left here is sufficient to guide only the most active of imaginations.

Sifting through scattered records like these is a one-way action. We have the records, *they* are the targets at which the records point. I am using these records in a way never intended by the persons I am searching for, and that acts as a valve, allowing the pursuit to flow in a single direction. The hunting party builds a fire to cook a meal. The Indian tracker reads the fire and the campsite as a set of directions to find the party. They did not leave behind the fire pit and the campsite in order to guide others to them; but they are there, and can be used for another purpose. If the party knew the use being put to such items, they could construct a story with them to lead, or perhaps to mislead, the ones who might read it. If the tracker knew that the hunting party might try this, the vocabulary of the message rachets up another level, where the intended and unintended parts of the message would have to be sorted out in order to find the usable parts. If the ones being followed knew that their intention to mislead might be perceived, they could construct a story at a level higher, and so on, spiraling up the semantic ladder.

But this way lies madness and literature. In the end, the power to be the perceiver, the right to have the last word, always lies with the tracker. He makes the choice by which he will be led or misled. For myself, I choose the assumption that these ancestors were not worrying about me searching for them a century and a half later. If I suspected, for even a moment, that Ebenezer and Aurilla knew they would be followed in this way, and had edited their behavior to affect its outcome, it would change the game. The person who would track *me* a century from now, after all, will be playing the game at a different level than I am playing it, since I conduct my life in the more self-conscious segments of the social spectrum. I plan my immortality. I even leave deliberate messages. And, sad to say, I mislead. I am constructing a story that, instead of being about what I am, is about how I see myself. Perhaps because I question the motives of those who would later pursue, I guard an area of myself in a delicate opacity, hidden by layers of misdirection. I do some of this intentionally, but even if I did not explicitly think about this future person, I would be committing the act of editing my life simply by giving this description of my own thoughts. Walt Whitman, in "Crossing Brooklyn Ferry," muses, "Who knows, for all the distance, but I am as good as looking at you now, for all you cannot see me." Is it any wonder modern critics have trouble focusing on the real Whitman?

And so I look through these records at Ebenezer and Aurilla and assume that they do not see me. The price I pay for making this assumption is that what I uncover is as unconscious as a mounted specimen on a microscope slide. This is the paradox of what I am doing this week. I would hear a message, have a visit. Can what I have made with my own hands, however, come alive and tell me what I do not already know? These ancestors did not leave behind them one picture, one poem, one parable, one story, which, shot through with a bolt of self-consciousness, might come to life in my Pygmalion hands. What I have is as cold as marble. I need a Venus to intervene and bestow on the data the self-awareness which has been excluded by the very means used to collect the information. But such miracles are not impossible. My imagination has played the god more than once.

Naiveté

Sunday brings a blustery wind from the southeast and the low, quick clouds of spring. After breakfast I stand outside of the motel to make the day's acquaintance. Because I stayed in place for the weekend a weather system has caught up with me. It wasn't exactly nipping at my heels, though: this front probably tracked up the western edge of the Appalachian chain. Many years ago I lived in a region like this, about a hundred miles from here, in upstate New York. In the spring of the Woodstock year I remember watching these same clouds tumble from one horizon to the other and thinking how close they were, and how much the enclosing land and sky gave the impression of standing in the bottom of a large, lidded bowl. I was a prairie boy who had always known the heavens to stretch the land. To have space compressed by the blue canopy was a great incongruity then. Now it seems more natural.

Yesterday was a frustrating cull through a mountain of subtle detail. It appears that Ebenezer and Aurilla owned the land they lived on in the south part of the county, though I won't be able to confirm this until the courthouse opens tomorrow. The highlight of the search was the large ledger books containing the tax records of the county in the period that the Luthers were around. Someone had the foresight to transfer these from the courthouse to the genealogical archives. Tax records, unlike land records, do not share in the metaphysics of ownership. The records of taxes paid by owners only have to be kept long enough to satisfy whatever legal mechanisms might have recourse to the events being remembered. A century-old tax record is of little use to the process of government. Over the years many of these records have been lost or discarded. They can be quite valuable to ancestor hunters, however. These accounts show that Ebenezer paid taxes on about twenty acres of land in Fairfield Township from 1847 to 1859. Judging from the tax amounts, Ebenezer was small potatoes in the local economy. The tax records take on more significance because of the lack of census records. The family came here after the 1840 census, and left just before the 1860 census. Only the 1850 census could have noticed them living here. Unfortunately Ebenezer and Aurilla are nowhere to be found on the census lists. People do get skipped, so missing names do not mean missing people. However, I found three of their children, ages eleven to fourteen, living on farms with other families in 1850. Probably Ebenezer, Aurilla, and the younger children were away the summer of the census.

Also missing is any overt sign of New York connections. The single pointer I found in Illinois takes on more significance now. There is probably some evidence of the earlier New York residency in the details, if I only had the time and the patience to unravel the knotted threads of social and family relationships. People then seldom relocated on a whim, or moved into a region where they had no friends or kin. But which of these people were socially connected to Ebenezer's family was not made clear by my light skim over the data yesterday. In this case it might be easier to work from some potential New York names. This is a segment of the trip that wants to flow the other way, from east to west.

Gusts of wind whirl old leaves and papers widdershins around my legs as I stroll to the car. This is Hamlet's southern wind, and it carries away the wild, antic disposition of the northwestern air mass. I am local, poetical, concrete. There is nothing on the agenda today. No travel, no research. It is a token of my middle age that these days have become more than short pauses between loud sentences. The visual and logical break between sentences is as much a part of discourse as the words themselves. They are the valleys that make the hills, the oceans that make the continents, the space that makes the stars. There is a good deal more of this nonstuff in the universe than there are things punctuated by it. Happy is the person who does not live only on land, or dwell only on a planet, or speak only words.

My mind is on Ebenezer and his family, and it is not. I have a notion to do two things today, or perhaps nothing. The day will lead and I will follow. I get in the car and let it move me south. Ten miles from here is where they lived. I take the back roads because they aren't convenient. If I needed more proof that I was no longer in the plains, the roads themselves would speak volumes. They twist and bend, rise and fall, perhaps following paths as old as the primeval cultures. I drive along copse and field, by houses that are modern and well kept, by trailer houses and poor shanties. Civilization sits lightly here, an afterthought.

When I reach the township where Ebenezer raised his family I am surprised to find an Amish settlement. I pass one or two buggies. They were not going the same way; this must be a visiting Sunday for one of the congregations. I can see the Amish influence in the farmsteads. Here are well-maintained houses and barns without the ugly power lines. Girls with head coverings and boys in plainsuits play in the farmyards. There are many more outbuildings on these farmsteads than in non-Amish settlements.

It is logical to find the Amish here, now that I think about it. The Amish seek out good, farmable lands on the edge of the American culture of progress. They want to be overlooked. Backwater regions are the places to find them.

There are more Amish in North America than one would expect. Nearly 100,000 last time I checked, surely more by now. They have large families, and most of the children—over ninety percent by one count—stay with the life style. One historian in the 1970s claimed that they were the fastest-growing Protestant religious body in the United States, all by means of the evangelism of procreation. There are not many individuals reared outside of their culture who have managed to become Amish. You can live with them as a visitor, even for a lifetime, but only your children or grandchildren will truly belong.

In the scheme of things that sees the society of North American people as linear and progressing along a single cultural track, the Amish do not fit. They do not feel protected by our armies, or expect to find justice in our courts. They opt out of our power grids, our elections, and our educational system. They do not want to share its costs, and they do not hope to receive its welfare. This quest for separateness has many times been to their harm. From them we learn that the easy pluralism of the American dream is more rhetoric than fact: the more clearly we have seen ourselves as people with a purpose, the more intolerant we have become toward those who overtly reject that purpose. Times of war have been especially stressful for the Amish, as we have sought to visit a share of the national distress on those who have not taken up the sword with us. We have perhaps been less intolerant, on the whole, than other nations. The Amish have tried—and still try—other countries. There are many of them in Mexico and Argentina, for example. But over the long run this is where they have remained and, when things have fallen apart, returned. It may be that we have been less sure in our national purpose than other lands, more experimental. Contrary to their image in the public press, their sojourn with us is not threatened by our attitudes of progress—over the last two hundred years they have been able to adapt to our enthusiasm for novelty. Their attitude toward the tools of progress is not merely negative. They do assimilate novelty—slowly, to be sure, but continually. But their future among us is not secure. What can undo them is reactionary certainty. They cannot build a culture that will resist such certitude without undermining their own existence. It has been the general lack of such certainty in the American experience, I suspect, that has made this land a place for them to thrive.

When I think about the Amish I do not think a single, focused thought. Their existence is as colorful and complex as you could imagine. The word *simplicity* has been applied to them too often. It doesn't fit. They are supposed to be a simple people, living close to the land, and avoiding the complexity of modernity. If *simple*, however, is the opposite of *complex*, then they are definitely not simple. The social warp and woof of an Amish community encodes an intricate design. A friend who lived in England told me about a dinner for an outgoing Master of one of the Cambridge colleges who complained, after forty years, that he still hadn't figured out how the university was run. But the lines of institutional authority at an English university are a child's drawing compared with a map of an Amish social network. Contradictions abound. Their church life is at once deeply theological and almost entirely noncreedal. They maintain an independence through concrete, communal assent and not through abstract denials based on hardy individualism. A better word than simplicity for their stance might be *naiveté*. Naiveté allows these contradictions, simplicity doesn't.

The word *naive* has taken on a negative connotation in the last century and a half. The more extreme Romantics discredited a serviceable word. The core sense of the word signifies the absence of malice, the lack of an intention to deceive. In coming back to this antique era this was one of the many conceptual boundaries I crossed. This word was headed for purgatory in 1840 and didn't know it. At the same time its wayward cousin, *expedient,* was scheduled for a parole hearing. When people in this age called a thing expedient, they meant it as an insult. They wanted to say that it was something short of sincere, or that it was of questionable moral content. We use the word today with commendatory overtones. Naiveté, on the other hand, once a state to be desired, seems less attractive today.

When I referred to the photographs of Solomon Butcher as naive, this older sense of the word is the one I was talking about. The photographs are not simple and uncomposed. But they are straighforward. The very artlessness of his art permits the people in the photographs to speak for themselves. When he set out to deceive, he made his deceit transparent, so that it would not interfere with the dialogue introduced by the person viewing the picture. His fiction is the comfortable artifice of a fairy tale. You cannot look at his pictures as pictures without feeling the silliness of a hypercritical stance toward them. They beg to be believed in, and not written about.

This is also the way in which the Amish can be called naive. They do not construct a version of themselves in relation to the natural world that must be defended at all costs. They have made themselves sensitive with respect to changes in their natural and social relationships. Sitting on a tractor and riding over the field makes it difficult to hear what the land is saying. A crop which cannot fail, because of fertilizer, pesticide, herbicide, or irrigation, is not a gift, exchanged by free parties, but an extortion from a captive earth. If a welfare system frees you from dependence on your neighbors and kin, you do not have true family or community. Taking up arms against an enemy also makes the social environment artificial. Their pacifism comes to just this: you cannot know the enemy as a full person if your opening gambit is a technological thrust of power. Enemies you can have, but only ones which are not, by the very conception of them as enemies, forced outside the possibility of interpersonal love.

The Amish are great believers in folk medicine. They doctor both in modern hospitals and at the welter of paramedical spas. Herbs and potions, and the lore of these, are infused in the social consciousness. They are extremely superstitious, and use a mixture of aphorisms to guide the major decisions of their farm life. These beliefs are all, again, a mixture of their naiveté, a part of their dialogue between their personal and social lives and the natural surround.

The Amish seem at first glance to be *deliberately* naive, if such were possible. If you were to map their social and technical expressions against a historical background, you would probably place them in the period I am in now, the 1850s. This can be misleading, however. The Amish themselves do not consciously aspire to historical re-creation, and can hardly see the similarity between themselves and the pre–Civil War farm society when it is pointed out to them. And so it should be. It does not matter to them that any particular piece of dress, or social practice, should superficially resemble that of another era. If it did matter to them, they would be as much slaves of fashion as some of *die Englisch*. They are the children of all days, keeping what fits and leaving what doesn't. Their naiveté is not programmed, in spite of appearances.

There is, nonetheless, a resemblance between Ebenezer and Aurilla and the Amish folk occupying their land these many years later. It is not an external resemblance of farming practice, dress, or social customs. It has to do with the version of the Great Experiment in which Ebenezer was, in the years of his prime, a participant: Ebenezer belonged to the Transitional era in North American history, a time when the interplay of civil life was being learned and celebrated, a time when religion was coming to grips with a world that was embedded in a political and social matrix which it could not fully control. There was a freedom to experiment which led to a multitude of religious, social, and political expressions. Technology was not yet the encompassing, dominating paradigm that it has become today. You did not have to believe or disbelieve in a technological dispensation in order to apply a technological device. Total war, just becoming a European practice, was not a feature in North America; the political baseline was a gentle anarchism. The similarity between these people and Ebenezer comes from the way that they share the social postures of the Transitional era. There was a considerable stretch of time, some forty to fifty years, in which the Amish perspective was also the interpersonal, concrete, and naive mind of much of the North American farming community. In this sense, then, the Amish witness to us a part of ourselves. They bring to us a remembrance of another attitude that is part of our common heritage. It is a similarity, not of flesh, but of the spirit.

This continent has been the home of more than one extended social experiment. A couple of days ago I talked about three versions of the Great Experiment. The ages with which I identified the experiments, the Foundational, Transitional, and Modern, are sequential, but the experiments themselves did not end with their ages. As each new experiment is set up, it joins the living members of the ones already in progress. The history of this continent is, then, an experiment of experiments. Perhaps the point of all of this social transformation, if there is a point, is to place side by side the outcomes of several efforts to define a working paradigm of the religious, political, and educational partnerships, and then to ask which one, in the long run, will be an answer to some of the pressing social questions raised by the contradictions of western civilization.

That the Amish are still among us makes them, by the strictest of calculations, a modern people, no matter how anachronistic they may seem. Their social life evolves. Their use of the land may be that of an earlier economic system, but their vital social relationships are not so easily passed over as an outmoded framework. They have delivered to us not only the testimony of our past but also a social order being reshuffled, reapplied, and reinterpreted for a later day. They are an ongoing experiment. In this they are not alone. The homesteaders of the early Modern nation were also an experiment, one which, to my thinking, compares poorly in its results with the one being conducted here by the Amish. Henry would not have understood what the Amish were doing with this land on which he spent his childhood, I think. But Ebenezer might have.

Revival

Today I move on to New York, emerging, for the first time in this trip, into a land where the Mississippi system has only a small role. Upstate New York is hydrologically ambiguous. A lot of it drains into the Great Lakes system, and on to the St. Lawrence River and the northern Atlantic. Another part leans toward the Atlantic through the Mohawk-Hudson system. On the southern edges there is considerable flow into the Susquehanna and then into Chesapeake Bay. A southwest corner siphons into the Allegheny River and thence into the Ohio and Mississippi rivers. With all of these systems to interconnect, it is easy to see why New York was where the canal boom of the early nineteenth century had its early expression.

Before I leave Meadville I stop at the courthouse to check the official records. One daughter of Ebenezer and Aurilla died here during the Civil War as a young woman, I notice. She was only thirty. But she was living on her own, on land purchased in her name, so there was a tiny probate. As I suspected from my work in the library on Saturday, Ebenezer was also a landowner, but only for the last few years he was here. The picture is of a family with no resources who moved in as laborers and over a period of time earned barely enough to buy a miniature farm. They were good candidates for going on west. One bad year, one serious accident, could have wiped them out.

More than this is not to be found in the official records. These few pointers, and some small contribution to the local gene pool, is all that is left from Ebenezer's stay. What else there is to know is in New York. I'm on the road before the morning is over. I've been to Buffalo before, however, in search of this family. Nothing turned up in those earlier searches, and nothing may turn up today. But I come equipped with a little more information this time. I now know that I should be looking in the western part of Erie County.

I am going down, as I travel north and then east, to the 1820s and 1830s. At the end of this stretch I will emerge in the heyday of the Erie Canal and the place of the first mass westward expansion by the new American peoples onto a piece of prime real estate. After lunch I will pass through the end of the world.

The Appalachian ridges, which flow up and down the western edge of the original Colonies, whose crests reach for hundreds of miles from east to west, were the first geographical barrier to the westward expansion of the European settlers. There is nothing particularly daunting about them. They were always a porous barrier. Settlers in small numbers had moved into them many years before the American Revolution. The staccato extinction of the titles of various Indian groups caused a stumbling sort of movement from the point of view of the land records. The problem with the Appalachian regions—the Alleghenies, Catskills, Blue Mountains, and such—was that the immigrants could not practice in these mountains the kind of farming, or create the kind of communities, that they knew on the coastal plains of the East. They came to the Appalachian areas in great numbers in the last half of the 1700s, but many, perhaps most, did not come to the mountains to stay. Some of the settlers adapted, of course, and they and their descendants became the Appalachian people we know today. Many of those who stayed were from the hilly knobs of the counties in the north of England and south of Scotland, and these mountains were to their liking. But the ones who would bring their technological, progressive civilization to the rest of the continent had their eyes on the land over the Appalachians. The first big prize was upstate New York.

The most politically cohesive of the Indian nations, the Iroquois, held dominion over the Mohawk and Genesee valleys and the plains south of Lake Ontario until the American Revolution. The longhouse tribes were farmers, and knew the value of the land they held. As long as they were in possession, no great number of settlers could make it their home. Intense pressure was put on them to yield their western Eden. By the 1790s the door was open, and into upstate New York poured a pent-up flood tide of Yankees. It was the best new farm land to be opened up in half a century. James Fenimore Cooper, whose stories are mostly about this dash into upstate New York, notes that, at the end of the American Revolution, New York had less than 200,000 people, and they occupied only ten percent of the land inside the state boundaries. He observes in the first of his Leatherstocking tales that by 1823 "the population has spread itself over five degrees of latitude and seven of longitude, and has swelled to a million and a half inhabitants."

Most of what was to happen in the succeeding century of westward settlement happened in miniature in this part of New York. It became the first great inland breadbasket. Wheat from here traveled to all parts of the United States, Canada, and the world. Into this region came industry, in all sizes and shapes. Here experimentation with railroads and networks of canals established the value of easy bulk transportation to local economies. The fires of religious revival swept across this land. In the Genesee and surrounding areas were born or nurtured many of the modern North American sects. Some, like the Mormons, the Wesleyan perfectionists, and the Adventists, were destined for success and expansion; many others flashed and died in the place where they were kindled. So intense were the flames of revival, and so often did they sweep through, that the area was known to church groups as the "burned-over district." Also from here, and related to the religious conflagration, came some of the early progressive political movements. Feminists and abolitionists and temperance workers strove for the allegiance of the same souls. This was, if you like, the California of the Transitional era. It was the Great Experiment at work, transforming religion and society. The word "experimental" was once used in contexts where we would say "experiential" today. When the folk in New York spoke of "experimental religion" they didn't mean to imply that their faith was held lightly. The Great Experiment here embraced both the ancient and modern senses of the word "experiment." The vigor of religious and social movements was both a testing of the waters and an inner, emotional assimilation of new social directions.

It is called the "second awakening" by the historians of American religion. The first awakening was the religious fervor at the end of the Foundational era. The ministries of Jonathan Edwards, George Whitefield, and John Wesley were part of a surge of religious awareness which resulted in the emotional transformation of tens of thousands of nominal Christians. After 1790 the smoldering fires reignited at the edge of westward advance. The settlers pressing into the Genesee and taking up lands along the new Erie Canal brought with them the coals of this fire. Charles Grandison Finney and hundreds of other itinerant evangelists and home mission workers helped to fan the embers into a searing flame with their "new method" approach to revival and conversion.

For twenty years intense combustion gripped this region. As the force of heat can catalyze the transformation of elements into new compounds, the fires of the second awakening gave rise to new religious sects and political movements. Upstate New York must be American holy ground. Anyone on a pilgrimage here should remove their shoes for a while, and look for burning bushes. The religion of the Foundational era in the Colonies hugging the Atlantic shore was a transplanted, and not a native, faith. The churches tried to play the role they had always played in the European homelands. The wrenching personal transformations inside the church door during the first awakening were carefully channeled into rigid cultural directions outside the door. In the second awakening, however, the church doors swung open. Through the door, and into this area, came experiential modes of Presbyterianism and Congregationalism. Methodist and Baptist churches spread through the whole region, and grew faster than wet corn under a hot July sun. By the time the revival had died down in the 1840s, the middle classes in the central and north of the continent had accepted evangelicalism and free churches as full members of the American household of faith.

Ebenezer must have been a part of all of this. When he was in Illinois, family tradition says, he was a member of the Free Will Baptists, one of the most experimental of the experimental sects to flourish within the bounds of orthodox protestantism. It seems certain that the family brought either this sect, or a sympathy for its belief and practice, from the eastern homelands. If I would encounter Ebenezer, I must look here. What I cannot know about him as an individual, I can know about him through his social matrix.

To see the construction put on a single life by the spiritual eruptions in this region we can have recourse to the spirituality of members of the congregations of these revived sects which are still with us. Even as the Amish survive, and even thrive, on the margins of the mainline culture, and witness to us an alternate attitude to family, land, and society, so the spiritual descendants of these revived Yankees have settled into our cultural backwaters. There are with us still, by the millions, Mormons, Adventists, Holiness sects, Evangelicals, and the like. Whether by fertility or evangelism, they grow and divide and multiply more quickly than the population as a whole. Their concerns may not make the nightly news reports, and their issues are not often spread across the daily newspapers, but they live quietly among us, and carry on the traditions and attitudes which were born in the fires of the second awakening.

Unless we come to some understanding of the dynamics of the surviving exemplars, we will remain isolated from the people of the Transitional era. The problem with the current expressions of these movements, however, is that the way they shape themselves is related to a newer version of the Great Experiment. We are studying the source of a river by watching it pour into the sea. A river means one thing where it has gathered up the kinetic force of a continent, and another thing where water sources gently mix on the height-of-land before being tipped onto a watershed. In this region was a spiritual ambiguity to match the hydrological ambiguity. It was a subtlety that I was missing in trying to find Ebenezer in the contemporary expressions of the churches of the second awakening. For I sought him there, even before I knew him. But I did not really know him, I realize, until I met William Miller.

But that is a story for the afternoon. I find the most expensive restaurant I can for lunch. No more french fries.

Millennial
Dreams

The wind pulls at the car as I move along Interstate 90 and the southern Lake Erie shore to Buffalo. Not many years ago this was a mangled stretch of highway, threatening to shake a car to pieces. Pennsylvania must have found the cash to put their share of it into shape. In its damaged state the road was like the bad roads on this side of the Alleghenies in the first fifty years of settlement. It is easier to understand the mania for canals in that era when you consider how bad the roads were. In the year 1840 there were over sixty canals under construction on this continent. Those tame waterways, though slow, were the smoothest of roads. What a shaking our passion for speed has brought us.

The Civil War is now so far over my head that its tumult makes little disturbance. There were prophets in the 1840s who saw it coming, but even then there were so many alternate routes to the present that no one could have known, with any real certainty, that the probabilities of the other pathways would shrink to nearly nothing, and that the cataclysm of war would engulf the optimistic and pastoral people of the Transitional era. Upstate New York in the year 1843 was more concerned with the imminent end of the world. The social and political problems that would eventually lead to war were no match for the excitement of the apocalypse.

The announcement of the end of the world in 1843 and 1844 was brought to the churches by a group we call the adventists. Their titular leader was William Miller. Father Miller, as he came to be known, traveled across these lands for more than twenty years with his message of hope and doom. Until just before the expected end of the world at the Second Coming the Miller-ites were not a separate sect; they worked within the newly revived Protestant churches. They would have thought it odd, in 1840, to see their eschatological concerns separated from the other aspects of their piety. And yet today such is our fascination with their millennial dreams that we hardly notice how continuous were their beliefs with the whole context of Christian practice at the time of the second awakening. They were not, until late in the game, a clique of heterodox social misfits. They were, on the contrary, the very embodiment of the enthusiastic Protestant spirit of the age. No one knows how many of them there were. At least 10,000 were core Millerites, but as the circle widens into the broader Protestant culture it becomes impossible to draw sharp lines. Perhaps 100,000 leaned toward the message at the center of the circle in a way that affected their faith and practice.

It is possible that Ebenezer had something to do with them. The Free Will Baptists, with whom he associated in Illinois, were enthusiasts for adventist ideas in the 1830s. If Ebenezer had been part of the Baptists when he was in New York, he could hardly have remained unaffected. When his son Henry brought the westering part of Ebenezer's children to Saline County in Nebraska they joined the Church of God. After the failed apocalypse many of the Churches of God were reconstituted out of the remnants of disappointed adventists. That Henry should feel comfortable in this church may mean that he had picked up adventist enthusiasms as a boy. He was seven years old at the time of the projected Second Coming in 1843, old enough to have shared the hope of his parents, and to have trembled at the descriptions of apocalyptic destruction which was soon to fall on his head.

When I was a young man I also had a brush with a modern version of adventism. The specific numbers and calculations and the order of events at the predicted end of the world are gone from my mind. I can hardly recall how the times divide. But I remember with force the piety, the emotional state, induced by my fascination with a terrible, imminent apocalypse. This memory is the lens through which I see Father Miller, and it is, I trust, a more reliable guide to what he was, and how it felt to believe what he did, than all the external speculations of history and theology. There is even a kind of apostolic line which connects the one form of adventism with the other: many of the Adventist Christians, especially those who had not let their millennial hope separate them from the new orthodoxy of revived Protestantism, dropped into the background, redid their calculations to remove the offending dates, and entered the twentieth century with Scofield Bibles and dispensational charts. Millions of North Americans today could explain the signs of the times as carefully and as competently as one of Father Miller's people could parse the prophecies of Daniel. In the 1970s books on the new adventism sold millions of copies. The attitudes of today's denominational bodies toward the new adventists is similar to denominational attitudes toward the first adventists in 1840. If they can keep their calendars under control, they are home and welcome in most Protestant groups and in the social framework derived from the second awakening churches.

Father Miller is hardly known today, yet for most of a century his message was part of the mainstream North American culture. For twenty-five years adventism was a rising, challenging player in the competition for the allegiance of believers. For the next half-century the beliefs of the adventists were kept alive through novels and through oral transmission in popular culture. In the beginning they were respected for their piety and devotion to the Scriptures. In the end they were a byword, a name used to conjure up human foibles.

The quietness of obscurity may be preferable to the vilification of fame. I should leave the dead to sleep in peace. I can no more rescue Father Miller from his fate than I can recover Judas from the place assigned to him. Yet these fundamental stories are sometimes the ones most in need of retelling. I will visit Father Miller.

William Miller had two dreams. Together they bracket his tragic life like a pair of finely carved bookends. The first one came to him at the beginning of his adventist labor. The dream was a complex trip through a naturalistic dreamscape filled with tableaux from Christian parables. At the end of it he came across two paths, one broad, along which many people were traveling, the other narrow and difficult. He took the difficult road. It does not take a prophet to tell the meaning of the two paths. In the second decade of the nineteenth century, Miller, having passed through stages of skepticism and deism, and having arrived at a place of status in his Vermont community, returned to the pious, awakened core of his Puritan tradition. He started to spend many hours closeted with a Bible and a concordance. Lacking the sophistication of a formal education, he interpreted the texts he was reading as practically and literally as possible, trying to make some coherent story emerge. Since no ecclesiastical divine was standing over his shoulder telling him that he should not try to make consistent sense of the lengthy sections of apocalyptic material in the Bible, he studied these with the same spirit with which he had approached more popular passages. When he began to include expositions of the prophecies of Daniel and Revelation in the Bible class he was leading, he could sense the alarm and excitement these unfamiliar texts aroused in his Baptist community. Back he went to his study, trying to understand what he had missed. But the same meaning was there, and the numbers added to the same totals. A conviction gripped him that he might have been called to make clear a part of the Holy Book which had been hidden to other generations. Had not the prophet Daniel himself said that the meaning of his prophecy was sealed until a later time? Were these perhaps the latter days, and had the time of understanding arrived? Miller, a shy man, fought for years with the thought that he had been chosen to witness these truths in the face of inevitable opposition from both the world and from his overly cautious church. He could not picture himself as a new Noah of the deluge of fire. In the end he acknowledged the calling and took his message on the road. This was the narrow path of his first dream.

At the end of his life Father Miller had a second dream. In that dream people came into his house and spilled on the ground the contents of his treasure chest, trampling the jewels and exchanging his good money for their counterfeit currency. Miller, in great agony over the loss, was unable to stop them. The valuables which were spilled were, of course, the adventist interpretations which had meant so much to him, and to which he had devoted the second half of his life. They had been spilled by people who had hypocritically refused to read the long apocalyptic passages of the Bible in the same literal spirit that they used when reading the rest of the Holy Book. His jewels had also been scattered by the relentless march of seasons, which, by the time Father Miller died in 1849, had overrun all of the dates he had set for the end of the world and annulled all of his predictions. Between these two dreams, the dream of the courageous pioneer and the dream of the lost cause, is a remarkable message in a remarkable time. The message came to be known in adventist circles as the *midnight cry*.

Without actually looking at the calculations themselves, it is difficult to convey the content of the cry in a way that captures its inner force. The computations are simple. Isaac Newton, who also spent the last part of his life decoding the numerology of the Book of Daniel, certainly did not have to employ any of the calculus he had invented for Kepler's ellipses. Millerites traipsed up and down New England with printed charts and primitive black-boards showing how grade school math could be applied to faith. The relevant texts take up the second half of the Book of Daniel. The basic calculation has to do with a dream of Daniel that 2,300 days would be needed to restore the "holy place." To Miller (and for that matter, to Newton and almost every other interpreter before 1860) Daniel's "days" signified years. Starting with the traditional date of 457 B.C. as the beginning of the restoration under Ezra, the Millerites subtracted this from 2,300 to get the A.D. date when the Second Coming would happen: $2,300 - 457 = 1843$. To bolster this main calculation, Miller used other numbers from Daniel which were commonly believed to relate to the papacy, and started these numbers running from events in the sixth century after Christ, events which were supposed to mark the inception of the medieval period. These also added up to 1843. Before he was done, Miller even had British victories over Napoleon worked into a grand plan of the ages. The effect of the convergence of these calculations was stunning. Consensus developed among the followers of Miller that the event in question was the end of the world, and that it would come sometime between March of 1843 and March of 1844 (allowing for the Jewish way of combining year and month reckonings).

Miller was initially worried about so unconditional a commitment to a single period of time, but he could not deny his own figures, nor could he deny the conclusion that life must be conducted in response to the facts of faith as literally interpreted. Expectation fueled the piety of adventism to a fever pitch in the final year of world. When the fatal year passed with no event, the Millerites convened a great conference, and, in a spasm of remorse, found what they thought might be the flaw in their calculations. Now a single date emerged: October 22, 1844. Again Miller and some of the more traditional Protestants in the movement fought the imposition of so specific a date. But they were caught in the grip of an impeccable logic. They could no more resist its demands to focus on a single date than they had been able to resist the temptation to confine the Second Advent to a single year. They could not, moreover, hold their people, and the attention of the public and press, with another vague year: something more dramatic was needed. Adventists and hundreds of thousands of others began to prepare for a cataclysm that would come on a single day in the fall of the year. Those who had reserves for the winter distributed them. Marriages were canceled. Crops were left unharvested. Some adventists who had lost dear relatives did not bury them, expecting them to be imminently resurrected. Businesses were neglected, stores were closed. No importance was attached to the campaigns of the 1844 election. Finally, on the fated day, devout groups gathered on hilltops, withdrawing themselves from the cities on the plain which were to share the fate of Sodom and Gomorrah. The desolation they felt when the minutes ticked passed midnight, and the corrupt earth remained unburnt and the pious people of God abandoned, can only be imagined.

By this time the mainline denominations had grown tired of the adventists. For the last year the Adventists had been separating themselves from even the evangelical Protestant denominations, expecting the lukewarm Christians who had not accepted the midnight cry to share in the judgment of unbelievers. Some of the churches began the process of reading them out of the congregations. Many nominal adventists found their way back into the fold, but many also abandoned their ties to orthodoxy in other areas of Protestant doctrine, and ended up in a variety of strange political and religious movements. But for all of them, leaders and followers, the menu was crow, and lots of it, for a long, long time.

This is the canonical version of an American tragic myth. But there is another interpretation of these events which does not fall so hard on Father Miller. Let me be one of his disappointed flock, and salvage what I can from the wreck of his prophecy. As a first move I step back to the reasons behind the logical grip of the millennium on his imaginative mind. It is a vantage that puts Father Miller in a better light.

The ideas of earlier generations of American religious thinkers, when they turned to thoughts of the end time, ran along less cataclysmic lines. They could be classified today as *postmillennialists*. For a postmillennialist the events surrounding the end of creation and the Second Coming were deferred to a time following a long period of improvement. The great events— the resurrection of the dead, casting Satan into Hell, and so on—came at the end of a millennium of gradual improvement, during which the church brought to the earth the blessings of the Kingdom of God. In this way of looking at the latter days Father Miller would be called a *premillennialist*. He looked for a great war and the arrival of Christ to come first, followed by a fruitful (but not unopposed) reign of God on earth, and terminated by a kind of massive wrapping up, the end of earth and time. These pre- and post- interpretations are not divergent in most major details. The main difference lies in whether you believe that the saints, without the intervention of tangible heavenly reinforcements, can usher in the millennial reign. The Puritans of the Foundational era were more sanguine about the influence of the church. The church that they knew already had control over major aspects of political and social life. It was not unthinkable that it would continue to maintain its sphere of influence, and even to extend it. The idea of the manifest Kingdom of God in the Foundational era looked a lot like an expansion of the Puritan commonwealth.

For the revived saints of Father Miller's time the outlook was not so cheerful. The Transitional era had seen the rise of a new American culture in which the secular sphere of political life and the domain of religious influence were on a more equal footing. It gave the church a different perspective. There was a possibility that the transferral of authority away from the church, already viewed with considerable alarm, would continue. It seemed utterly remote that the mixed allegiances of Americans might develop into anything resembling a glorious millennial period. Thus the steps into the millennium were not likely to be gradual ones. Nothing short of a major assault by the armies of Heaven could bring the saints into a strategic placement where a genuine millennium could begin. The prophetic mind of Father Miller was acutely aware that the church was in the waning days of its period of major influence, and that the times were in transition to a culture of political power and secular learning. He could see on the horizon the dawn of an age in which none of the old formulas worked. He could see the first light of a time when Americans would not share the Puritan expectation of a religious commonwealth. Out of this vision, and his agony over its losses, Father Miller's premillennialism was born. There was a need for a major intervention. When Daniel's prophetic numbers added up, the stage was set for a reinterpretation of the apocalyptic drama foreseen by his Puritan forbears. Christ would return first, and bring the reinforcements needed to reverse the implacable forces dragging the nation into a secular future. Then would come the millennium. This was the perspective of pre-millennialism.

There was, of course, no Second Coming in the way Miller had predicted it: the day arrived and passed without the hoped-for events. The problem with Father Miller's interpretation was not with the clarity of his vision, however. He saw the future in finer detail than his contemporaries, who were, for the most part, sleepwalking into the most violent, ambivalent period in American history. Without some kind of drastic intervention, he realized, the experiment as he had known it would veer off into a dire and unpredictable direction. Miller could not stop it alone. The solutions of his contemporaries were impossibly small bandages on a major hemorrhage. They could not, by themselves, and with their puny communities and ineffectual rhetoric, counter the Lord of Battles that was coming into the land. The leader of the new forces was a god of war. He had come to sweep from his land the political vestiges of the old world, the slavery and aristocracy of the Old South, the claims of Britain to Canada and the Pacific Northwest, and the Spanish monarchy from the southwest. He had come to clear the land of the Indians before the advancing waves of western settlements. And all of this he would do in a mere thirty years. His people would inherit the land, from sea to sea, and millions of immigrants would flood through its gates to believe in his gospel and to fill the waiting lands.

Did Father Miller, riding his horse through the wilderness of upstate New York on his journey from one lecture to another, look over the newly cleared lands and see these changes in the Great Experiment? And did his gaze lift higher, reaching perhaps up to our own time, and see the commencement of a global reign of nuclear law in which the values and customs of this people would become the standards of an empire, just as the Romans spread the language and patrician attitudes of a single state to the ends of the known world? For Father Miller, this domain of the Lord of Battles would be a counterfeit millennium. If he could have believed in it—and I fancy he must have tried, the irenic man he was, to put himself in a place where he did not need to call down heavenly fire to fulfill his hopes—he could have saved his dates and his reputation. He had the time right. It was his allegiances that betrayed him. His commitment to the Christian version of the millennium was too strong. He could not renounce the parts of his belief that contradicted what his prophetic vision saw. He could not bring himself to stop believing that the meek would at last inherit the earth, and that the first might really be last. He could not bring himself to believe in a kingdom that was built on the backs of the poor. Could he see that two hundred years later only one out of every fifteen people would be living inside the walls of the City of God and its suburbs, and that the other, impoverished fourteen would be in the Third World? If he could have, it would have made him more of an opponent of the new order than he already was, and more certain that divine intervention must come swift and soon.

From this visit with Father Miller I can take away one gift, but another I have to leave. The one I must leave behind is the florid imagery of his literal apocalypse. For most of us the sense of the Puritan commonwealth and its deeply religious ideals has receded so far that, even if we accept Father Miller's diagnosis, we do not have a large, countervailing framework on which our hopes can repose. The new adventists can voice our fears, but they do not tell our hopes. Our faith, such as it is, comes wrapped in smaller packages.

The gift I can accept from Father Miller is that of his reaching vision. I view with him the alteration of the Transitional experiment and the beginnings of the new order. We have lived under the domain of the Lord of Battles so long that we find it difficult even to focus on the character and quality of that earlier social order. An infection had taken hold of Father Miller's contemporaries. Miller saw it in its earlier, insidious stage. It turned out to be typhoid, however, and the rack of civil war, though it did not destroy us, left us changed, left us to reconstruct a new experiment out of the ruin of the old. But the time dividing the two experiments cuts along, and not only across, the grain of time. There are with us those whose hopes and values and ideas are more consistent with that earlier experiment. They are there in the woodwork, living in the backwaters, amphibians who remember the days of slow canals and fresh water, a time of careful husbandry of the land, and the era of spiritual enthusiasm. To have seen this is, in some measure, to have believed in the vision of William Miller. To this extent I am, I suppose, a Millerite.

By a turn of irony the Union troops, in the act of putting an end to the Transitional experiment as the dominant social paradigm, would march into battle with a counterfeit millennialist hymn. Julia Ward Howe's "Battle Hymn of the Republic" was a paean of joy to the Lord of Battles. "Mine eyes have seen the glory of the coming of the Lord." But here, on the holy ground, where the fires of revival burned and the kingdom was announced, and not on the blood-soaked battlegrounds of Gettysburg and Antietam, was the Lord's field, and here was His threshing, years before anyone believed that the kingdom could be won with the marching and bivouacs of earthly armies.

Eire County, New York

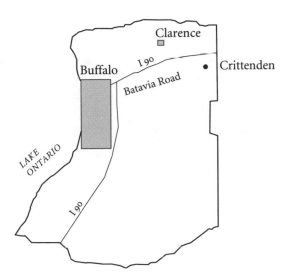

Erie

Tuesday, the ninth day. There are several places in Buffalo where I can consult genealogical records. I start at the Greek Revival temple of the historical society. It is a place which has known too many genealogical researchers. All of the access systems for the library have been planned in fine detail. You sign in, pay your fee, and receive a printed description of the holdings and a short tour of the indexes from one of the staff. When you use the collection, most of the resources you want to consult must be fetched by a librarian's assistant. If you find something you would like to look at in one of the indexes you fill out a slip. When they are not too busy, it is about ten minutes between slip and book.

This situation reflects a more advanced stage of genealogical organization than anything I have seen this week. It is a common pattern from here to the east coast, representing a compromise between the goals of preservation and needs of the unwashed hordes of hobbyists. The price I pay for having access to a lot of perishable sources in one building is the inconvenience of finding any particular piece of information in those sources. Some members of the staff in these places are not genealogists. They know the library procedures, but they don't have either time or inclination to talk shop. When I'm not allowed to browse the shelves, some types of searches are more trouble than they are worth. My impression of such places is that they are depersonalized factory systems set up to handle greater numbers with minimal budgets. Bird watchers must feel this way when they go out to nature centers on weekends and find themselves walking heel-to-toe with long lines of birders, all carrying binoculars and notebooks. Still, it's hard to imagine any other way to handle the problem represented by numbers.

I wonder how many local genealogists still meet here, and consider this a social hub of their research. Several of the essential tools are almost worn out by decades of use. The census lists are nearly unreadable from the scars of too many trips through the microfilm readers, for example, and pages are loose in key reference books. The approach to fragility in this library is to restrict rather than to replace. As I poke among the indexes and reference shelves, the sensation of a certain era emerges. My guess is that the heyday of genealogical research in Buffalo occurred in the 1940s and 1950s, a period that corresponds to the generation after Buffalo's last boom. The surge in the western New York economy in the 1920s would have brought new people into the upper circles of Erie society. One of the last expressions of a social caste moving through a system is the marrying phase, where new money weds old money. Each of these marriages brings new branches to the family tree which have to be explored, sanitized, then dignified with honored placement in the halls of ancestry. Genealogists, it would seem, sometimes inhabit the same decadent, twilight space as philosophers.

After lunch I move my research to the county records building. For my morning's labor I am no further ahead in the search for specific data about Ebenezer, but my sense of what it would have been like to live in Erie County when Ebenezer was here is enlarged. The 1830s were probably Buffalo's finest days as a port city. This town is the essence of boom and bust. Its highs were higher and its lows were lower, and the time between these shorter, I think, than any city of comparable size.

On the way I stop at the public library to use the census microfilm collection. These are slightly easier to read than the ones at the historical society. The new information on Ebenezer has paid off. I find him on the 1840 census in Alden Township. I back up ten years and look for him in Alden and the neighboring townships: no entry. So Ebenezer and his family were not here for long. They came from somewhere else in New York. The name of Erie County descended in the family as the New York location, then, because the oldest children spent their childhood here, but not necessarily because this was Ebenezer's home.

This library has the same printed census indexes that I used in my earlier search for Ebenezer. Out of curiosity I look at them to find out why they didn't point me to Alden Township before. The index has misspelled his name! I remember reading a study of these census indexes which suggested that up to twenty percent of the entries were botched. This is a dangerous tool. It had broken in my hand, and I didn't know it.

The county records office is similar to the records offices in the county seats of the Midwest, just more aisles and more ledgers, reflecting a longer history and a larger population. The older records, now relegated to the basement, are still open to public access. I know from an earlier trip that Ebenezer does not show up on the land records—that is, if I can trust the deed indexes. My faith in indexes has received a shock. I had better spend some time doing linear searches, now that I know the approximate dates.

Nothing turns up on Ebenezer. I do find one passing reference to his brother John in a court case, but the original documents are missing from the box. Perhaps I have just paid the price for using an accessible tool. There is another way I can go, though, to get a fix on Ebenezer. Contiguous names on a census list often represent neighbors. By tracing neighbors it is possible to locate where someone was living even when specific land transactions for that person are missing. Some of the neighbors are bound to have been landowners and to have generated records with survey locations. The trick works. Ebenezer is probably living on the old Batavia road, a major thoroughfare in Erie County in this period. In checking the ownership patterns of the farms in that vicinity I discover that there is a small, fifty-acre farmstead on this site whose first purchaser, in 1838, was Lorin Wait. This must be a close relative of Aurilla, perhaps a brother. He held the land until 1847, which is the first year that Ebenezer and Aurilla appear on the Crawford County tax records. This is probably the reason that I have not had any luck with the land records: Ebenezer and Aurilla were living on an in-law's land when they were here.

The trail becomes overgrown now. Certain tracking techniques might take me further. It may be possible to turn up the name of Ebenezer's ancestors. Aurilla's family might be easier to trace eastward, however: I notice that there are other Wait names in the eastern Erie County records.

That trail, however, is another trip, a research trip. Were I to follow that tangled path now, it would end the pilgrimage. Before long I would be fighting my way through the underbrush, merely collecting, and not trying to see what it means. Old inhibitions of the researcher about going beyond the evidence would rise up to suffocate my imagination. Pilgrimages should not end by being frittered away with the press of other demands. I am at the limit of my safety line. Ebenezer and Erie County were given names, part of the line reaching from Nebraska to here. If it is to reach further I must construct it first. Building lines, however, is not the same as following them. The terminus of this line is a small piece of rural Erie County real estate about twenty miles east of Buffalo. Before the day is over I will find that land, and, finding it, end the journey. Tomorrow I yield to the many small goals which have been forced to the edge of my consciousness in order to open up the pilgrim space.

The New York tollway takes me to within a few miles of the place. On the maps is a small town, called Crittenden, close to the site. When I arrive, there is hardly anything there suggesting a town. The few buildings are old, and seem more like farmhouses than town buildings. This was a place where two roads crossed in the last half of the nineteenth century. A small knot of tradespeople huddled together. There was probably a school and a church. Farm land was gradually subdivided into smaller and smaller lots so that more homes and businesses could be accommodated. At some point they platted a town. Looking at a map drawn up after the Civil War, I can count about twenty buildings which would have been absorbed into the town. As traffic on the road decreased, everyone but those actually making a living from the land moved away. Today there is little hint of the town that was here a hundred years ago. This is like Algernon. I imagine that even the school has been moved.

I park the car so I can walk around some of this territory that Ebenezer must have known well. Spring has taken hold in the last two days. This is drying weather. Even a week ago my foot might have depressed the grass an inch at every step. Now there is a firmness pushing back against my tread. The sog and sovereignty of mud is nearly over. In one week I have come from the last throes of winter to the edge of summer, down through a hard springtime of typhoid, gambling fever, war, and failed visions. My pilgrimage has brought me to a warming, late spring land in the Transitional nation.

According to the history of Custer County, Nebraska, Solomon Butcher had an inventive streak. When he first opened up his portrait studio he could not afford a new backdrop. He used the only large cloth which he had, the one that had covered the Conestoga wagon that brought him to Nebraska. It was as soiled and patched as the clothes he wore. As a result, his studio portraits inadvertently recorded the sorry state of his financial affairs. So he hung the backdrop from the ceiling by bedsprings. When he was ready to take a picture he would give the cloth a sharp pull, then quickly rush to make the portrait before the backdrop stabilized. The time required to make the exposure on those ancient glass negatives ensured that anything moving too quickly was blurred. The imperfections of the backdrop disappeared in the resulting portrait.

The Transitional era in which Ebenezer lived, and of which, I suspect, he was a fairly typical representative, is like that sad cloth. To value it requires a change in the viewer, a slower shutter, a naive glance that lets in enough of the natural light both to construct the edges and textures of the human image in the foreground and to blur the background. Our better roads and progressive spirit have, however, acted like a faster shutter. They have made the backdrop seem tawdry. They have drawn our attention from beauty in the older social form.

Ebenezer was, I think, a less stubborn, less certain man than his son

Henry. He was, I believe, a person with a rich emotional life, a dreamer of dreams so big that he could not bring them to fruition. He knew both the quiet moving of the soul and the excitement of the spiritual fires burning in this land. He neither sought nor found the stability of material success. I doubt that his immediate children, who became part of another era, understood him. And that, perhaps, is the reason they forgot him, the reason why the dynastic title descended to his son. I do not know whether I have understood Ebenezer either: a nine-day pilgrimage is not a long time next to the span of his life. The glimpse I have had of him on this trip is based on too much reconstructed evidence. The light of imagination, probing the fog of probabilities, sometimes creates the images it seeks. There may be more of myself on the negative than there is of him. But I have the picture, and it is better for the extended exposure. Later I may see in it a detail that escapes me now. Just in case, I have written it down.

Sources

Text pages to which the sources pertain are listed in the left-hand column.

vii   Jonathan Messerli. *Horace Mann*. (New York: Alfred A. Knopf, 1972) 586.

3   Henry David Thoreau. *Walden*. In *The Writings of Henry David Thoreau*. 20 vols. (Boston: Houghton Mifflin, 1906) 2:29.

15   The most extensive discussion of Kem I have been able to find is DeLloyd John Guth. "Omer Madison Kem: The People's Congressman." Master's thesis, Creighton University, Omaha, Neb., 1962.

18   Geoffrey Marks and William K. Beatty. *The Story of Medicine in America*. New York: Scribners, 1973. The number of typhoid cases during the Civil War is discussed on p.247.

19   Sir John Conybeare, ed. *Textbook of Medicine*. 9th ed. (Edinburgh: E. & S. Livingstone, Ltd., 1950) 45.

20   A. B. Christie. *Infectious Diseases: Epidemiology and Clinical Practice*. 3d ed. (Edinburgh: Churchill Livingstone, 1969) 68.

25   John Carter. *Solomon Butcher: Photographing the American Dream*. (Lincoln: University of Nebraska Press, 1985).

36   Willa Cather. *My Ántonia*. (Boston: Houghton Mifflin, 1918) 5.

52   Lillian Schlissel, Byrd Gibbens, and Elizabeth Hampsten. *Far From Home: Families of the Westward Journey*. New York: Shocken Books, 1989.

76   Donald Culross Peattie. *A Prairie Grove*. (New York: Literary Guild of America, 1938).

90   Michel Chevalier. *Society, Manners and Politics in the United States: Letters on North America.* [1836]. Trans. T. G. Bradford. (Garden City, N.Y.: Doubleday and Company, 1961) 297.

91   Francis J. Grund. *The Americans in Their Moral, Social and Political Relations.* 2 vols. (London: Longman, Rees, Orme, Brown, Green and Longman, 1837) 2:8.

94   Albert Bernhardt Faust. *The German Element in the United States.* (New York: Arno Press, 1969).

97   Alfred North Whitehead. *Process and Reality: An Essay in Cosmology.* (New York: Macmillan, 1929).

100 Henry David Thoreau. *The Maine Woods.* In *The Writings of Henry David Thoreau.* 20 vols. (Boston: Houghton Mifflin, 1906) 3:95.

102 Burton R. Clark. *The Academic Life.* (Princeton, N.J.: Carnegie Foundation for the Advancement of Teaching, 1987). The chart of the growth of faculty at U.S. colleges and universities on p.12 of Clark's book is derived from the *Digest of Education Statistics: 1982,* U.S. Department of Education.

103 Garry Wills. *Under God: Religion and American Politics.* (New York: Simon and Schuster, 1990) 383.

105 George W. F. Hegel. *Philosophie des Rechts.* The translation of this Preface sentence is from T. M. Knox, trans., *Hegel's Philosophy of Right.* (London: Oxford University Press, 1952) 13.

113 Captain Basil Hall. *Travels in North America in the Years 1827 and 1828.* 3 vols. (Edinburgh: Cadell and Co., 1829) 1:147.

115 Eugene Lemire, ed. *Unpublished Lectures of William Morris.* (Detroit: Wayne State University Press, 1969). This quotation is from Morris's "Early England" lecture, first given in 1886.

118 Walt Whitman. *Complete Poetry and Selected Prose.* Ed. James E. Miller, Jr. (Boston: Houghton Mifflin, 1959) 119.

130 James Fenimore Cooper. *The Pioneers.* (New York: Penguin Books, 1988) 16.